WHAT PEOPLE ARE SAYING
COURAGEOUS MARKETING
AND UDI LEDERGOR

"This book offers a smart, compelling argument for boldness in B2B marketing. Udi Ledergor lays out a clear, practical approach to standing out in a crowded field—without gimmicks or empty hype."

—DANIEL H. PINK,
#1 *New York Times* bestselling author of *To Sell Is Human*

"This book contains a blindingly different and important recommendation for marketers: Don't stay clear of all risky situations. Rather, cultivate them selectively, armed with a well-resourced plan to channel them into major successes. Best of all, it tells us exactly how to develop such transformative plans."

—ROBERT CIALDINI,
New York Times bestselling author of *Influence* and *Pre-Suasion*

"Great marketing stands out and sparks action. *Courageous Marketing* uncovers how winning startups build bold brands, ignite conversations with thought-provoking content, and transform customers into raving fans."

—NIR EYAL, bestselling author of *Hooked* and *Indistractable*

"*Courageous Marketing* challenges the safe, conventional approach that keeps so many brands invisible. Udi Ledergor shows how daring strategies and thoughtful risks can transform not only your marketing—but also your career."

—MICHELLE TAITE, CMO at Intuit Mailchimp

"We need more courageous marketers to turn the tide on uninspiring B2B marketing. If you're struggling with getting engagement on your content, events, or brand campaigns, this is a great playbook."

—NEIL PATEL, Co-Founder at NP Digital

"I don't know about you, but I'm tired of playing it safe. And there is no better person to teach us how to be bold than Udi. Why? He's lived it. This book cuts through the b*llsh*t and shows us how to challenge the status quo and build brands people can't ignore. Don't stop. Don't question. Just buy it."

—KYLE LACY, CMO at Jellyfish

"Modern marketers are expected to make an impact on strategy, content, events, and brand campaigns, to name just a few areas. *Courageous Marketing* provides inspiration and practical advice on how to excel in each of these. Udi Ledergor also shares crucial steps you can take to advance your career in marketing and thoughtfully build an empowered team that acts as a force multiplier."

—**TRICIA GELLMAN**, CMO at Box

"Creativity will forever be the most important ingredient to a successful marketer. This book gives you permission to take chances and stand out. Study it."

—**DAVE GERHARDT**, Founder of Exit Five

"Finally, a marketing book that shows *how* to take risks to get outsized rewards. Udi Ledergor delivers a masterclass in building memorable brands with vivid examples and actionable frameworks. This is the guide I wish I'd had early in my career."

—**CARILU DIETRICH**, CEO & CMO Advisor

"As a VC, startups are always asking me for advice from top GTM leaders. Udi is my #1 go-to for all things marketing. His proven, modern approach is a game-changer for companies of all shapes and sizes."

—**MAX ALTSCHULER**, General Partner at GTMfund

"Every CMO should read *Courageous Marketing* because it's packed full of contemporary, practical marketing wisdom with real-life examples from well-known companies. Most importantly, it challenges CMOs not to end up in Davy Jones' Locker at the bottom of the Sea of Sameness."

—**DAVE KELLOGG**, EIR at Balderton Capital

"An effective marketing team needs more than creative campaigns. It needs to make sales easier and align with the sales team to achieve shared goals. *Courageous Marketing* clearly breaks down the elements and processes for doing both of these things extremely well."

—**RYAN LONGFIELD**, VP of Americas Revenue at Shopify

"In an era where AI will increasingly filter and summarize our marketing, brand and human connection matter more than ever. Udi Ledergor shows us how to break free from 'safe' marketing to build the kind of lasting brand equity that transcends algorithms and drives sustainable growth. *Courageous Marketing* is a must-read for any marketing leader ready to make their marketing truly matter!"

—**JON MILLER**, Co-Founder of Marketo and Engagio

"Working closely with Udi for six years taught me the foundations of standout marketing that cuts through the noise and drives measurable results. With *Courageous Marketing*, now everyone has access to Udi's bold, inspiring marketing strategies. Don't think twice, you won't regret reading this book."

—**CHRIS ORLOB**, Co-Founder & CEO, pclub.io

"Many claim to have the playbook for B2B marketing, but only few can truly speak to building a category-defining brand from scratch. Even fewer have the courage and vulnerability to share the experience openly and pass the knowledge forward. *Courageous Marketing* does just that—with the right amount of self-awareness and humor, making it a must-read not just for marketers—but for every tech leader."

—**OMER RABIN**, Co-Founder and CRO at Anyword

"Marketing mediocrity is insanely competitive. It's the battleground of every average marketer—and every new AI approach. But as Udi describes in practical detail, it takes courage to reach beyond this morass and take bolder swings that can pay off in awareness, affinity, and affection."

—**ANDREW DAVIES**, CMO at Paddle

"*Courageous Marketing* is not a book written by people analyzing the game, but by people in the game. It's a playbook filled with experiences written by marketers for marketers. You can pick it up, read one story, and immediately take inspiration from real tales of building a great business."

—**RUSSELL BANZON**, CMO at Cresta

"In a world where playing it safe feels easier, *Courageous Marketing* is a refreshing call to embrace bold, fearless marketing. Udi brings years of hard-earned wisdom having built one of the most important enterprise software brands of our time, offering real, relatable insights that inspire us to think differently and lead with purpose. If you're a CMO ready to break through the noise, this is the guide you've been waiting for."

—**ANTHONY KENNADA**, Founder of Goldenhour

"I had the rare privilege of creating highly effective marketing alongside Udi Ledergor for three years. During that time, I experienced firsthand the impact that courageous marketing had on our brand and sales pipeline. It's remarkable that Udi managed to squeeze in so much practical advice into such an easy read. Every marketer looking for inspiration will find it in here."

—**DEVIN REED**, Founder, The Reeder

COURAGEOUS MARKETING

THE B2B MARKETER'S PLAYBOOK FOR CAREER SUCCESS

UDI LEDERGOR

COURAGEOUS MARKETING
The B2B Marketer's Playbook for Career Success

For permission requests, speaking inquiries, and bulk order purchase options, email inquiry@actionableideaspress.com.
P.O. Box 27126
San Francisco, CA 94127
UdiLedergor.com

Author Photo by Nir Arieli
Editing by Lori Lynn Enterprises | LoriLynnEnterprises.com
Design by Transcendent Publishing | TranscendentPublishing.com

Digital ISBN: 979-8-9921784-2-5
Hardcover ISBN: 979-8-9921784-1-8
Paperback ISBN: 979-8-9921784-0-1

Printed in the United States of America.

"Creativity takes courage."

—Henri Matisse

To Guy, Tom, Noa, and Adam.
You are the source and inspiration
of my courage.

CONTENTS

CONTENTS

FOREWORD

B2B marketing has become a sea of sameness: stock photos of people shaking hands in suits, 40-page whitepapers, and yawn-inducing webinars. Boring, canned, and stale.

Companies know they need to stand out, but most don't know how. And now, with the rise of Artificial Intelligence, the challenge is only growing.

The old playbook? It doesn't work anymore. Buyers aren't making decisions based solely on product specs, pricing, or vague promises about "revenue generation." Instead, they're gravitating toward brands with personality, clear values, and the courage to be different. This isn't just about looking cool; it's about staying relevant. Companies clinging to outdated marketing risk becoming invisible.

Why? Because even in B2B, decisions are emotional. Buyers want to feel something when they engage with a brand. They want to trust it, connect with it, and believe in it. But far too many B2B companies are afraid to take risks. They stick with safe, bland marketing, hoping not to rock the boat.

As marketing leader Udi Ledergor will tell you, playing it safe is the riskiest move of all. The companies thriving today are those that dare to break the mold, embrace creativity, and make bold choices.

This is why his book *Courageous Marketing* matters so much. Udi gets it. He knows how hard it is to break free from the status quo, and he's lived the journey. He doesn't just preach bold marketing—he's done it.

I've known Udi for years, and I've seen his impact firsthand. He helped transform Gong from a promising SaaS startup into a brand people love—a brand they root for. He did it with bold campaigns, fearless creativity, and a clear vision. Gong isn't just respected; it's adored. And that's no accident.

But Udi's impact goes beyond Gong. As a teacher, mentor, and inspiration, he's shaped the careers of countless marketers, including many in Pavilion, the global community I founded for revenue professionals. His classes at Pavilion's CMO School are consistently top-rated because Udi doesn't just talk theory—he gives real, practical advice that gets results.

I am a passionate believer in the power of brand and the impact that a truly differentiated brand can have on a company's growth. There's no better evidence of that power than Udi and his incredible career building iconic brands. Udi challenges us to think differently, push boundaries, and build brands that ignite raving fans.

I'm proud to call Udi a friend and collaborator, and I couldn't be more excited to see his insights captured in this book. *Courageous Marketing* is a guide for anyone ready to ditch safe, stale marketing and create something remarkable. This book lays out the blueprints for exactly how to do that with boldness and, of course, courage.

If you're ready to create a brand people care about—one they truly love—this book is for you. It is a must-read for every CMO.

I hope you enjoy it!

—Sam Jacobs
Founder & CEO of Pavilion
Co-host of *Topline* podcast
WSJ bestselling author of *Kind Folks Finish First*

FROM MUNDANE TO MAGICAL

"Often, in the real world, it's not the smart that get
ahead but the bold."

—Robert Kiyosaki

Jerry Maguire isn't the only one demanding, "Show me the money!"

Every board of directors, CEO, revenue and finance leader is pleading with marketing teams to do the same. Marketing doesn't exist to win creative awards or provide jobs (although those are helpful byproducts). Marketing—especially business-to-business (B2B) marketing—exists for one main reason. And if you get that one thing right, it's like having career insurance.

Great marketing makes sales easier. It's that simple. Show them the money and everything becomes infinitely less complicated. At its best, marketing is a force multiplier, fueling the well-oiled sales machine. So why does it fail so often?

Look at most B2B brands and you'll find yourself yawning at a swamp of mediocrity: boring stock images, bland color palettes, and messaging that sounds like an AI regurgitation. After studying hundreds of B2B brands, speaking with dozens of Chief

Marketing Officers (CMOs)—several of whom I've interviewed for this book—and serving as the CMO of Gong from 2016 to 2023, I've discovered a few common reasons why marketing efforts tank.

From playing it safe through death by committee and lack of product-market fit (PMF), to ignoring the long-term game, there are different reasons why marketing fails.

You might have brilliant ideas for taking your company from zero to hundreds of millions in revenue in a few years (like we did at Gong). But if you play it too safe or subject your ideas to death by committee, you'll never realize your full potential or your company's.

Cows kill more people than sharks every year[1]. ("I'm surprised cows kill any sharks at all!" goes the old joke). Death by committee will kill far more marketing efforts this year than all the cows and sharks ever could. When you try to please everyone, you get caught in the cycle of never-ending opinions. That's not a place of action or innovation. But if you've got a great PMF and can make bold long-term plays while speaking up and taking a stand, you've got a solid recipe for recurring marketing success.

We'll discuss ways to overcome common obstacles, when to speak up, and how to present crazy ideas to create remarkable marketing. You'll discover frameworks for succeeding in everything from brand building, through content marketing and event experiences, to unlocking your full career potential while building a high-performing team.

---

[1] Jade Eckardt, "Fact Check: Do Cows Kill More Humans Than Sharks?," Surfer, July 24, 2024, https://www.surfer.com/news/cows-kill-more-humans-sharks.

More importantly, you'll uncover what courageous marketers do to create careers they are passionate about while building iconic brands.

You'll gain practical insights and actionable strategies from the brightest minds in marketing, such as Dave Gerhardt, Carilu Dietrich, Tricia Gellman, Anthony Kennada, Michelle Taite, and Andrew Davies. These leaders helped build iconic brands like Salesforce, Drift, Atlassian, Box, Intuit Mailchimp, and Gainsight. They generously shared their experiences, lessons, and frameworks for success with me.

Through interviews with brilliant operators I collaborated with on building Gong, such as Ryan Longfield, Russell Banzon, Sheena Badani, Devin Reed, Chris Orlob, Jonathan Costet, and Vince Chan, you'll see what's possible when marketers dare to be courageous and work well with sales.

At the time of writing this book, I'm the Chief Evangelist at Gong, which employs well over 1,000 professionals globally and is still growing rapidly. While most of my experience and lessons are from the B2B startup and scale-up space, many of them are valuable and applicable to other company types and stages.

From building and leading marketing teams at highly successful companies, advising dozens of others, serving as a board member and angel investor, and mentoring hundreds of startup founders and marketers, I've learned that the marketing world is rapidly changing.

Most startups don't get a seemingly overnight success story like we've built at Gong. Believe me, I get it. In fact, I've been there. I know most B2B marketing sucks. And that's why I've combined what I've learned from my decades-long marketing career into this book. I hope it inspires other marketers to create visionary, courageous marketing that truly moves the needle.

The purpose of this book is to help you create a movement of raving fans around your brand and grow a successful business by engaging prospects, customers, and employees. I know from experience that courageous marketing leads to predictably scaling demand generation and brand awareness while responsibly running creative experiments.

I've discovered strategies, tactics, and secrets of finding your courage as a marketer, creating an iconic brand, grabbing mindshare in a noisy market, and appearing to be much further ahead than where your company's really at. This makes prospects believe they're buying from an established brand, which makes sales and marketing a lot less challenging.

Whether you're a startup founder figuring out your first marketing hire, a CEO setting goals for your marketing team, or a marketer aspiring to transform from "meh" to "wow!" you're in the right place. This book will help you find the courage to take action on those seemingly hair-brained ideas that could command the attention your company deserves.

Are you ready to create an iconic brand for your company? Become the talk of your industry for effective marketing? Earn a seat at the management table for *showing them the money*? Then have the courage to read on!

CHAPTER 1

A SUPER BOWL COMMERCIAL?

"Boldness be my friend."

—William Shakespeare

"Your neck is on the line," read the email from my CEO.

It all started a couple of weeks earlier, on a frosty San Francisco night in October 2020. I was the CMO at Gong, an early-stage startup helping sales teams close more business by capturing insights from their customer conversations.

My CEO, Amit Bendov, who was based out of Israel, traveled into the city. We met for drinks at a trendy rooftop bar. As our second round arrived, I took my shot with one of my crazy ideas.

"So I've been thinking about how to elevate our brand in a big way that would set us apart from the competition."

"I'm listening." He lowered his drink.

"You know how big consumer brands take over the Super Bowl commercial breaks?" I treaded carefully.

"Sure." He furrowed his brow. "But those spots cost millions of dollars—our entire annual marketing budget!"

"Turns out we can buy regional media where our target audience is," I grinned, "at a fraction of the cost of the national spot."

"I love it!" Amit raised his drink as his face shifted from puzzled to mischievous. "We're having dinner with our CFO tomorrow night, let's twist his arm there and get him on board."

Our glasses clinked as we toasted our plan.

The next day, we approached Tim, our predictably skeptical CFO.

Amit led the charge with enthusiasm. "Udi got us a great deal on a Super Bowl commercial!"

Naturally, Tim had a list of questions, but we answered each one with the confidence that comes with extensive preparation. We were both surprised when he didn't put up much of a fight after seeing how excited Amit and I were about elevating our brand in such a substantial way. We assured him that the investment would be minimal because we intended to buy a regional spot and develop a marketing campaign around the well-placed ad.

The next step would be going before the company's board of directors to ask for their approval. You probably know that Super Bowl commercials are a battlefield of marketing creativity usually reserved for business-to-consumer (B2C) brands. Few business-to-business (B2B) brands have made the risky investment in the big game, and for good reason. It's difficult to target the right audience, not to mention measuring the performance of the steep investment.

Many board members consider this a form of vanity marketing that can't be financially justified. So I had to be careful about the way I positioned it. I explained that this was a long-term brand play and that we were not expecting to see any short-term moving of the needle.

Amit emailed our board: "Udi and I believe it can make an impact ... and will help elevate the company's profile. If it does not make an impact, we will not repeat it in the following year. It is worth trying."

One after another, the board members responded with hesitant approval. The last one signed off his email, "If we did not have Udi and I did not have confidence in him, I would say let's not do it but that's not the case."

Amit forwarded me the board approval thread with his succinct take on it: "Basically, your neck is on the line. Good luck."

Challenge accepted.

Not taking lightly the board's trust and budget, I set out to build an entire digital campaign to support this 30 seconds of very expensive airtime. We started one week before the game and we continued it a full week after the game.

My biggest hurdle was producing an effective commercial on a modest budget. When I asked a fellow CMO who'd produced several Super Bowl commercials to recommend a creative agency, he laughed me off. He didn't know anyone who could work with my tiny budget. I ended up trusting a small video production agency. They had never created anything at that scale, but I'd had positive experiences with them on smaller projects.

With scarce resources, I had to be very creative. Working through multiple COVID-related restrictions, we filmed a single actor at a furniture store over the weekend. The commercial had a somber humor to it, appropriate for the pandemic times.

We used a shooting style called forced perspective, which made the actor portraying a VP of Sales appear tiny in what looked like a giant, empty office. Remember the movie *Honey, I Shrunk the Kids?* It's kind of like that.

Borrowing a trick I'd used in email and social media campaigns, the first four seconds of the commercial featured a close-up shot of a "VP of Sales" nameplate on a desk, aimed at keeping our target audience glued to their seats instead of filling their Doritos bowls during halftime.

We shot the commercial in December, right before the winter holidays, giving ourselves January for editing and signing off, just before the Super Bowl deadline in early February. We barely made it.

Getting More Bang for Our Buck

We kept our commercial a surprise until game day. I was one of the first to share it on LinkedIn on the morning of Super Bowl Sunday 2021. Now, if I had paid attention to "best practices," I would have held off sharing until Monday. But I would have lost invaluable momentum.

Conventional wisdom says that Sunday is a terrible time to share something on a business network. But I discovered through this experience that Sunday works just as well as weekdays, if not better—as long as you've got something exciting to share. And we did.

It completely blew up on LinkedIn. People couldn't stop commenting. There were over a thousand engagements, and hundreds of comment and shares. People were going wild about it. If you haven't already seen it, you can watch the commercial online by going to this link or scanning the QR code below:

bit.ly/gongcommercial

SCAN ME

On Sunday and Monday, we got hundreds of thousands of views online once our employee advocacy campaign kicked into high gear. Hundreds of employees, whom we affectionately refer to as Gongsters, shared the commercial on their personal LinkedIn profiles.

To encourage our followers to share it with their networks and increase the buzz, we gave out free swag—200 special-edition Gong Super Bowl t-shirts. One of them has our mascot, Bruno the bulldog, in a football helmet (a role he landed after auditioning among seven other bulldogs). The other one has the helmet on the front and the back says, "Closer."

We posted the commercial on LinkedIn and promised, "If you share this and tag Gong, Vince from my team will send you a special edition Super Bowl t-shirt." Within a few short hours, hundreds of fans shared our commercial. By 11 a.m., the t-shirts were gone. My team ordered several hundred more t-shirts to keep the momentum going.

We also contacted our top 10 influencer-partners who shared with their social networks on Monday morning, giving us another huge audience. Our LinkedIn followers, mostly sales professionals, were bursting with pride. They couldn't believe they were being featured in a commercial during the most-watched game of the year.

What could have been a quickly forgotten 30 seconds of fame turned into our company setting a new all-time record. Evidence of our commercial's success quickly accumulated:

- New prospects reached out to learn about our product.
- Our Chief Revenue Officer reported that judging by customer calls with his team, our brand had been elevated in a major way.
- Using Gong's revenue intelligence software, I tracked hundreds of customer mentions of our commercial, confirming that our regional targeting had worked well.
- The cherry on top was that Super Bowl week marked a new all-time record for sales pipeline creation at Gong.

We had created more new business opportunities than in any other week in the company's history. Even I was surprised by how well my crazy idea had worked.

Describing our Super Bowl commercial, other marketing leaders called it "risky," "ballsy," and "a waste of money." But the courage I found to question common wisdom and act as few B2B marketers had acted before me paid off in spades.

Armed with inarguably positive metrics, I presented the results to my CFO. A data-driven person in every fiber of his being, he reluctantly agreed it was a brilliant investment on our company's behalf.

He even helped me secure a much larger investment for the following year's Super Bowl. Even though our company was a relative latecomer to the market, our brand grew so quickly that it went on to dominate the industry for years to come—despite our second commercial flopping (more on that later).

CHAPTER 2

THE RISKIEST STRATEGY OF ALL

"Playing it safe is the riskiest choice we can ever make."

—Sarah Ban Breathnach

"Why is there a bulldog on my log-in screen?!"

This question came from a puzzled customer reacting to the big visual identity launch I led at Gong in 2018, which was far from an established brand at the time.

As one of thousands of new SaaS startups, we knew we had to cut through the noise to grab our audience's attention. While most companies were using a limited, subdued color palette considered "safe," we took the opposite approach and went pretty wild in choosing our brand colors, mascot, tone of voice, and imagery.

The visual identity we launched became a sensation that inspired countless startups over the years. We didn't touch it again for more than three years. Then, in late 2021, after serving mostly small- and medium-sized businesses (SMB), we evolved our brand to better serve a new audience of larger enterprise customers.

We refined and polished some of the graphic elements to look more mature and less startup-like. We added crucial content around privacy and security standards, which our enterprise customers considered a must-have. We tightened the language to make it less casual, but we kept all the key components that made the original 2018 launch so successful (yes, we kept the bulldog).

Could I have avoided some harsh reactions by consulting with more people ahead of the launch, collecting feedback from a larger panel, and ensuring nothing in the new brand launch would be remotely offensive to anyone? Absolutely.

Would I have done things differently if I could go back in time? Not a chance.

Most startup operators believe that to gain trust as an authority in their space, they need to appear serious and thoughtful and constantly talk about their company, product, and achievements.

Open a dozen random B2B websites and social profiles and you'll find company awards, product release updates, and stock photos of handshakes in board rooms. It seems like these well-intentioned yet misguided marketers are confusing authority with stuffiness. This is a typical result of risk averseness or, in other words, "playing it safe" which, I'll argue, is the riskiest strategy of all.

The result is low engagement with their social profiles, weak website traffic, and brand awareness that hardly grows. Some companies manage to grow without great marketing. But for most startup brands struggling to stand out in a crowded market, choosing between boring and brilliant marketing could determine whether they live or die.

Brilliant doesn't mean eye-catching colors, a memorable logo, or unusual fonts. When it comes to the visual and creative elements, you have to remember that there are two components at play: the message and its packaging. But what's far more important than the package is the message.

You could have a plain, no-frills website—just black text on a white background—but if your message is clear and resonates, it could still work. On the flip side, a pretty website cannot make up for a bad story.

If you don't profoundly understand who your audience is, what their pain is, and whether your solution clearly solves that pain— even Apple-caliber designers won't be able to make it work. Get your story straight first, and then design around it.

As you're creating your messaging and trying to build your brand, I would caution you against getting *too much* buy-in from outside voices.

Death by Committee

"I've searched all the parks in all the cities and found no statues of committees," quipped English writer Gilbert Keith Chesterton (1874–1936). G.K. Chesterton would turn in his grave if he knew that nearly a century later, most marketing teams consult with company-wide committees in doomed attempts to create exciting brands and campaigns while trying not to annoy anyone too much.

In committee decision-making, the focus is naturally on consensus and compromise, which can dilute the creativity and innovation of the individual. Many marketers seek input and feedback from their peers, in an attempt to avoid conflict or surprise them with marketing materials they might dislike. The end result is over-involving them in the process, trying to appease each individual by working their input and preferences into the company website, whitepaper, or press release.

Anthony Kennada, a serial CMO and entrepreneur, has a good guess for why this happens:

> "Marketing needs to be a service organization to the sales team. So marketing solicits feedback from sales to ensure their support. This, in turn, creates a velocity problem when sales wants to weigh in on *everything* marketing does and gets upset when their opinion is ignored. Chasing ideas that come from sales or the CEO creates tension and a challenge for marketing to prioritize what they should be doing."

The result, more often than not, is a mediocre hodgepodge of ideas that won't offend anyone but is unlikely to excite anyone, either. There are two common flavors of this approach: targeting too many buyer personas and chasing after too many goals.

Too Many Buyer Personas

When you try to appeal to everyone, you end up appealing to no one. Think about it this way: which business email are you more likely to respond to—one that includes little or no personalization and could have been sent to pretty much anyone, or one that took care to address your current job title, top priorities, and timing within your annual business cycle? This level of personalization is difficult to get right for a single buyer persona. It's downright impossible to accomplish for multiple personas, at the same time, using the same email.

This happens more often than you might think. Carilu Dietrich, an advisor to CEOs and CMOs at hypergrowth companies, tells a cautionary tale:

> "One early-stage company I advised had traction in two very different industries with very different requirements. They couldn't meet the needs of both with their limited resources. To be successful, they had to pick a lane—an industry, a buyer, and a use case where they could be exceptional. This was the only way to really scale and grow. You can't be everything to everyone, especially when you're smaller."

Carilu helped them successfully scale demand generation *after* they picked one industry to hone in on.

Too Many Goals

Trying to achieve numerous goals in a single campaign or content piece will likely result in not achieving any of them. Meeting a single goal, such as maximizing the number of downloads of a whitepaper, is hard enough.

As soon as you start adding goals—increasing brand awareness, driving demo requests, advancing sales opportunities, and going viral on social media—you're unlikely to achieve any because your efforts are diluted and spread too thinly across too many objectives. Your campaign is no longer optimized for a single, clear goal. Your target buyers become confused about what they should do next.

When a buyer doesn't feel their needs are met in a piece of content, an event experience, or a billboard message, they walk away unsatisfied. That's the risk of trying to appeal to everyone: you dilute your message, resulting in bland marketing.

Committee work can be productive or deflating. Carilu Dietrich saw both extremes: At Atlassian, her team was maturing the brand ahead of an IPO. They came up with an advertising campaign that was liked by some folks and criticized by others. "We kept trying to get more unanimous love and kept trying new campaigns. In hindsight, we should have persisted with the first idea instead of changing it multiple times based on everyone's feedback," she said. "We would have benefited from the consistency and repetition of pushing the same message in the same way to the market."

Repetition is powerful, and perfection can be the enemy of progress. Everyone can criticize an idea but few can come up with better solutions.

At Oracle, Carilu had the opposite experience. The company spent millions of dollars on ads for the front page of *The Wall*

Street Journal and in airports around the world. The CEO at the time, Larry Ellison, was very decisive, which made it easy for Carilu's team to make progress. The consistent brand and consistent messaging made Oracle's red-bar ad—with messaging like "20 of the 20 Top [Companies]"—iconic, despite much less spend than IBM or SAP.

The CEO's decisiveness could be controversial—she remembers Larry giving their legal team exactly three lines at the bottom of their ads to include all disclaimers, regardless of how much they wanted to say. "Larry's philosophy was that legal can help us clean up if we get into trouble. They shouldn't block us from running the business effectively. Just think of how bad those pharmaceutical ads can get!" she said.

When a buyer experiences a hyper-personalized, cheeky marketing campaign that feels purpose-built for them, it's usually the result of a small team's work producing a single, engaging, sharp point of view.

Dave Gerhardt pulled this off nicely at Drift after agreeing with his CEO to name their new category "Conversational Marketing." "We rolled it out without going through six months of deliberations with a ten-person committee," he recalls. While the category didn't take the market by storm, the company did command a lot of attention to itself for its forward-thinking and engaging marketing.

Take in all the relevant input you can get from internal and external stakeholders, but make sure you clarify who the decision-maker is and that not all feedback will make it into the final product.

Avoid Playing It (Too) Safe

Anyone who's ever worked in the IT world is familiar with the saying, "Nobody ever got fired for buying IBM." It's a tongue-in-cheek reference to playing it safe in the mainframe world. Rather than risking your career as an IT professional and choosing an up-and-comer in the space, just go with the incumbent, and nobody gets into trouble.

Each of us has a different tolerance for risk, but in a high-stakes corporate environment, most marketers will play it safe, like the IT buyer who chose IBM. It's hard to blame them for taking what appears to be the safe route. After all, if they try something risky and it fails, they could lose the trust invested in them or even their job.

But playing it safe is often the riskiest path you can take as a marketer. Part of the magic of great marketing is being surprising, inspiring, and fresh.

Granted, we all need mental shortcuts to accomplish tasks faster. When we know others have faced similar challenges, we may be tempted to study and mimic the so-called "best practices" in the field so we don't have to reinvent the wheel every time we face a new challenge.

The motivation to model what appears to work is understandable, but the result is often lackluster. Why? Because by the time anything becomes a recognized "best practice," almost everyone is doing it.

We've all seen the stock photos of people shaking hands in meeting rooms and 40-page whitepapers nobody reads—except your competitors. In other words, ordinary actions deliver only ordinary results.

One way of avoiding blandness is speaking your buyers' language. Drift gained credibility by having marketers speak with each other, creating real dialog instead of a one-way broadcast. "Too many companies speak *at* their audience instead of *with* them," said Dave Gerhardt, who was the CMO at Drift. "Using third-person language instead of a first- or second-person voice alienates your audience."

I did this at Gong, too, hiring former salespeople to create content for other sales professionals, which created a lot of credibility and came off as authentic advice from the sales trenches.

Another risk-reduction tactic often used by B2C companies is polling customers on their preferences. Carilu Dietrich used this method effectively in B2B, often conducting customer roundtables to discover what resonates with her audience. "When communicating our decisions internally, we reduced the perceived risk by explaining that we're going with 'what customers want,'" she said. You can override your customers' requests with good justification, but making a data-driven decision is a safer way to hedge your bets.

With the right messaging, you can be bold with its delivery. With courageous marketing, you can elevate your company's brand and increase demand for your products and services in ways that will make your competitors' heads spin.

Start by staying keenly aware of when you might be playing it overly safe or letting good ideas die in committee. Next, we'll explore why it's important to make your company appear to be much larger than it really is in its early days and how to pull it off on a shoestring budget.

CHAPTER 3

PUNCH ABOVE YOUR WEIGHT

"He who is not courageous enough to take risks will accomplish nothing in life."

—Muhammad Ali

"How many employees do you have, about a thousand?" a guest asked me during Gong's 2019 Celebrate conference. His guess was fair since he'd seen our brand show up everywhere from billboards to his social media feed.

"Something like that," I smirked.

We had fewer than 200 employees at the time.

Great marketing makes your company appear to be much further ahead than it really is. Appearing to have more employees and customers is beneficial because most businesses, especially large enterprises, prefer buying from established companies rather than from young startups. The only ones who typically like buying from startups are the innovators, technology enthusiasts who love experimenting with new products, and early adopters who see the potential in new technology and are willing to take risks to use it.

In his book *Crossing the Chasm*, Geoffrey A. Moore explores how technologies are adopted first by innovators, then by early adopters, followed by the early majority, the late majority, and finally the laggards. The book's title alludes to the chasm between the early adopters and the early majority, which marketers can narrow or bridge to accelerate the adoption of their products and give their companies a chance to survive.

To become more attractive to early- and late-majority buyers, companies can appear to be bigger by pulling marketing stunts usually associated with larger companies. The Super Bowl commercial we discussed in Chapter 1 is an illustrative example. Most people assumed we paid $5 million or more for the in-game national television spot when, in reality, we paid a tiny fraction of that for three regional spots.

As Ryan Longfield, Gong's Chief Revenue Officer at the time, reported after the commercial aired, customers he spoke to thought of our company as being on "a totally new level" after seeing what *appeared* to be a multimillion-dollar television spot.

Advertise Offline, Amplify Online

Standout companies like Salesforce, Gong, Drift, and others have used this simple yet powerful campaign framework to create the perception of a much larger company:

1. Pick an offline medium typically associated with bigger companies such as a billboard, TV spot, or major print publication.
2. Buy a small, affordable version of your selected medium. This could be a small billboard on the outskirts of Times

Square, regional TV or radio spots, or the regional edition of a national print publication.

3. Get creative with the use of the medium for a campaign folks can get excited about. For example, you could feature a customer testimonial.

4. Photograph your campaign in a way that makes it appear bigger than it really is—like we did with the billboard surrounded by lively foot traffic in Times Square.

5. Share your photos and videos on the company's social media and other channels.

6. Activate employees, customers, and partners to share the campaign and extend its reach.

My team at Gong came up with a variety of cost-effective "real world" campaigns and then used our social channels to amplify them online. Since our followers were mostly Gong fans, engaging our captive audience with these campaigns would elicit excitement and social sharing, also known as "going viral."

Dave Gerhardt ran campaigns like this at Drift when he was the CMO. He recalls the time they bought out the Nasdaq Times Square billboard for 30 minutes and amplified it on social media. On another occasion, his team bought a small billboard next to an early customer's office and featured the customer on it. "They got so excited about it and had many folks share it on social media," Dave said.

At Gong, we pulled off the Times Square billboard trick many times. The iconic location always garnered interest and people assumed we spent an arm and a leg to advertise in this prime location. In reality, we spent as little as a few hundred dollars for rotating ads on a small billboard. We sent a photographer to capture our 15 seconds of fame with the hustle and bustle of Times Square in the background. We then amplified the photos and videos on social media to a much more relevant audience than the humble billboard could ever reach.

Paddle is a UK-based payment infrastructure provider, that took this idea literally out of this world by launching their software into outer space[2]. The core campaign idea was knowing that the business founders they served loved geeking out about space and the next frontier. As their business expanded globally, they thought it would be cool to expand it into outer space.

CMO Andrew Davies takes us behind the scenes: "We paid under $15K for the campaign, less than most companies spend on an ebook. We hired an agency to help us capture the whole thing on film but I hated the first cut. I wanted to crawl behind my sofa and disappear. So we filmed another whole day and combined that with the original footage to create something usable."

Andrew's team found a brilliant way of tying their brand investment into a demand generation campaign. They created 300 different videos showing how their prospects' payments could be processed anywhere, even in space, and made them part of an Account Based Marketing (ABM) campaign. Prospects who took a sales meeting with Paddle earned a personalized space jacket with a badge suggesting they had been to space.

The ABM campaign generated $6.5 million in sales pipeline. "This helped us break into accounts we had previously struggled to access," Andrew reflects. "As I travel the world, people often

---

[2] "Space... The Final Payments Frontier," Paddle, accessed January 25, 2025, https://space.paddle.com/.

point at me and call me 'the space guy.' A great side benefit was the swagger and courage it gave our team—it proved we could literally shoot for the stars."

During the COVID pandemic, my Gong marketing team and I realized we didn't need physical billboards to achieve our brand awareness goals. With everyone working from home and few people walking the streets, we commissioned a graphic artist to create virtual billboards and used Photoshop to place them in Times Square. While we didn't hide the fact that the images were digitally created, many followers assumed the billboards were real and got excited, especially when we featured our employees of the year on them.

Tricia Gellman, a serial marketing leader and advisor, took a similar approach to boosting brand visibility during her time at Salesforce: "Building a brand is not just about awareness— it's also about instilling confidence. At Salesforce, we always punched above our weight." Her team bought up all the advertising spaces on bus shelters and newspaper stands around their offices, creating the perception that they were much bigger and more well-known. This gave her employees a confidence boost, empowering them to speak with more authority to customers.

This localized media-buying strategy had measurable results for Salesforce, according to Tricia. She said, "We focused on a few cities where we already had good business momentum and made targeted brand investments there—at airports, on the radio, and on billboards. The impact was clear: we saw larger deal sizes in those cities."

At Gong, we applied a similar focus on strategic branding during the last fiscal quarter of the year. We took out a full-page ad in *The Wall Street Journal* to highlight how our software could help businesses forecast year-end results. Instead of paying for the pricey national edition, we opted for the more affordable West Coast edition. Once the paper was out, we photographed the ad and shared it on social media, achieving the same impact as if we had invested in the national edition—at a fraction of the cost.

One of our most fortuitous experiments happened during a San Francisco Warriors game. We tried a virtual overlay of our logo on the Warriors' basketball court. NBC sold us the ad space at a reasonable rate, and it aired in the San Francisco Bay Area. As luck would have it, Steph Curry broke his three-point shots record while hovering over our logo. The iconic moment was shared widely, Gong logo and all, by the Warriors, NBC, and Gong, exponentially amplifying its reach.

Warriors on NBCS
@NBCSWarriors

STEPH CURRY BREAKS RAY ALLEN'S RECORD FOR MOST CAREER 3-POINTERS

94.1K views   0:02 / 1:23

4:43 PM · Dec 14, 2021 · Twitter Media Studio

1,037 Retweets   166 Quote Tweets   4,067 Likes

These campaigns underline an important lesson: to appear larger than you are, focus on dominating a small geographic region where you can make a big impact. That's exactly what we did in the San Francisco Bay Area, where many of our customers were located. Had we spread our advertising budget thinly across multiple regions, we wouldn't have achieved the same outsized effect.

Employee and Customer Advocacy

When customers and employees share content and stories about your company, they're amplifying your presence. There are several ways to achieve this opportunity to look bigger than you are, and the beauty is that you can pull all of them off at a very low cost.

A good customer- or employee-advocacy campaign starts with creating content your customers and employees are excited to share. Chip Heath and Dan Heath serve excellent prescriptive advice for creating stories that stick and get shared in their aptly named book, *Made to Stick*. In a nutshell, they describe the six principles of sticky ideas: simplicity, unexpectedness, concreteness, credibility, emotions, and stories.

Your ideas are less likely to stick if the stories don't sound credible (although many bogus stories that *sound* credible still make the rounds). And if they're overly complicated, mundane, and don't evoke an emotional response, you've lost your audience.

The marketing team at Drift ran an effective employee advocacy campaign around a book the company published. They managed to get a distribution deal that placed their book in airport bookstores. Dave Gerhardt, Drift CMO at the time, recalls:

"Employees and customers traveling through these airports saw the book, took selfies with it, and posted them on social media. That got us a ton of positive buzz."

Customer awards are another great example of content your customers are likely to share, because who doesn't like recognition? It makes them feel proud, especially if you're already a somewhat established brand. To be sure, bogus awards have been overdone and should be approached with caution but, done right, awards make for effective content that customers love sharing. G2, the customer review platform, does an excellent job of getting their customers to share numerous awards each year, increasing their credibility and brand awareness.

Similarly, employee recognition targets your own employees. By giving them meaningful recognition (at Gong we call our employees of the year "Outstanding Gongsters"), you give your employees a chance to show pride in their workplace by sharing the recognition bestowed upon them and their peers. An added bonus is showcasing a company culture of recognition that increases job applications.

Your customers and employees are also likely to share any great piece of content if they think it will make them appear smarter, cooler, or on top of the latest trends. So why *not* design your content to achieve that?

Budgeting for Experiments

"How did you finagle a budget for those adventurous brand campaigns?" I am often asked. Any doctor will tell you that the best medicine is preventive medicine. The same applies to budgeting brand campaigns. During each budget cycle, I explicitly allocated 5–10% of my budget to a line item titled "Marketing Experiments" (although my team fondly referred to it as "Udi's crazy ideas").

Most of our brand campaigns got funded through that line item. From buying a huge billboard wishing our local employees a great day to Gong-branded food-delivery robots surprising prospects with pizza (hey, it was an experiment!), we almost always found a budget for fun ideas.

Every marketing team needs to experiment with new channels and campaign ideas to eventually replace its current channels because few, if any, can remain lucrative forever. An experiments budget also helps to exploit opportunities that present themselves during the fiscal year but were unknown during budget approval.

A classic example is an industry event you might want to participate in that gets announced after your budget is finalized. Most CFOs and CEOs will understand and agree with this logic, ultimately creating a budget cushion you can use for experiments, brand investments, and even as a small emergency fund.

I always assured my CFO and CEO that we treat experiments as a small-scale pilot for exploring a new channel or campaign idea. If it works well, we'll budget more for it; if it underperforms, we won't repeat it.

By including these marketing experiments in your budget from the get-go, you will find it much easier to get them approved on the fly, as you skip the "how will we budget this?" argument and focus on why you think it's a good idea and what business impact it could create.

Measuring Brand Investments

Ask any marketer to measure a brand campaign and they will admit how tricky it is. There is a well-documented mix of traditional methods, like before-and-after awareness surveys, and marketing attribution tools that give you an idea about the efficacy of your investments.

Companies like Paramark are using Marketing Mix Modeling and experimentation to help B2B companies understand incrementality, marketing measurement, and forecasting.

One overlooked way of gauging the impact of brand campaigns is using revenue intelligence software. "We used Gong to track customer calls mentioning our space campaign video, and it showed up massively," said Paddle CMO Andrew Davies.

I used the same technique to measure the impact of a podcast sponsorship. Michael Lewis is a prolific best-selling author, perhaps best known for his book *Moneyball*, which was adapted into the Brad Pitt movie of the same name. He has quite an audience, which allows him to charge a handsome amount for sponsoring his podcast.

When he offered to interview my CEO on his podcast for a five-figure dollar amount, many CMOs would have run the other way. This type of investment is notoriously difficult to measure: you might get some listenership data from the podcast owner but it's virtually impossible to cross-reference it with your own target audience, leaving you in the dark as to how many of those listeners are people you care about. But I had Gong on my side.

Gong's revenue intelligence platform captures customer interactions over phone calls, video conferences, and emails, analyzes them with AI, and surfaces actionable insights for revenue leaders. After I set up a simple Gong tracker, it identified dozens of customer calls mentioning the Michael Lewis podcast. This was the validation I needed that this investment was driving podcast listeners to request a Gong demo.

To estimate the impact of our Super Bowl commercial, I created another Gong tracker to uncover customer mentions of our commercial. This revealed hundreds of sales calls that provided the proof I needed: the buyers we cared about had watched our Super Bowl commercial.

Savvy marketers use an assortment of measurement tools like surveys and regional sales analysis to assess the impact of brand campaigns. The best teams add revenue intelligence to the mix as a measurement tool for brand investments like content assets, billboards, print advertising, radio and TV commercials, and events, all of which are difficult to assign marketing attribution to.

So there you have it: a simple-to-follow framework and plenty of real-world examples of how to make your company appear to be much bigger.

Having your brand perceived to be a couple of years ahead of where it really is can accelerate your business by attracting early adopters who don't typically buy from startups. Accomplish this by punching over your weight with brand campaigns that appear to come from a much larger company:

1. Pick an offline medium.
2. Buy a small version of it.
3. Get creative with the medium.

4. Photograph your campaign.

5. Share on your company's social media.

6. Activate employees and customers for extended reach.

Preemptively budget for these brand campaigns with an experiments ("crazy ideas") budget and add revenue intelligence to your marketing measurement mix to pinpoint your campaign audience.

Creating outsized brand campaigns is both effective and a lot of fun. Unfortunately, it's not enough. To build a successful brand, you need the entire company behind you or risk spectacular failure. More on how to navigate that challenge is waiting for us in the next chapter.

CHAPTER 4

YOU CAN'T OWN BRAND

> *"Your brand is what people say about you when you're not in the room."*

> —Jeff Bezos

Brand is too important to leave it to marketing.

Yep, I said what I said.

Now, I know what you're thinking: doesn't marketing *own* the company brand? Doesn't it get to decide what the company stands for, what it looks like, and how it sounds?

No, not really.

Jeff Bezos's quote holds equally true for people and companies, which raises the question: What *do* people say about you when you're not in the room? How do they decide what they believe about you, what they expect from you, and how they feel when your name comes up? Marketers' lives would be so much easier if people formed their opinions of our brands based on the snazzy slogan we used in our recent ad campaign. Unfortunately, it doesn't quite work that way.

As every parent knows, children do as parents do, not as they say. If you're a smoker, how credible do you think you sound when you warn your child about the dangers of tobacco? Company brands work the same way.

People form opinions and feelings about your brand based on how it shows up in the real world, far more than on your marketing campaigns. An old marketing adage reminds us that "perception is reality." So how do we build favorable brand perception?

One way we got the entire company to consistently uphold what our brand stood for at Gong was by developing a set of operating principles[3], which accurately described how we made decisions and operated. They were not aspirational cliches like "stay humble" or "act with integrity." Those types of corporate values end up on an HR poster in the office kitchen, only to have eyes rolled at them while employees wait for their coffee to brew.

We wanted to describe who we *really* were so we could attract like-minded candidates who would thrive at Gong and train new recruits on the way we do business. We even recognized team members who exemplified our operating principles at our annual awards ceremony.

One operating principle, which quickly became synonymous with Gong's culture, is "create raving fans." This principle is at work when a recruiting coordinator creates a fantastic experience even for a candidate who didn't get an offer (to the point that many of them write glowing reviews on Glassdoor after being rejected!). It is at work when a support rep goes above and

---

[3] "Our Operating Principles," Gong, September 13, 2023, https://www.gong.io/operating-principles/.

beyond to solve a customer problem, earning a high satisfaction score in the process.

When the entire company lives and breathes its operating principles and creates raving fans every day, *that's* what people say about you when you're not in the room.

You're the Party Host, Not the Club Owner

This is where marketing gets exciting. When an entire company operates like a well-oiled machine to create raving fans, everyone's job becomes easier, especially for marketing.

Former Growth Marketing lead at Gong, Jonathan Costet, experienced this transformation firsthand. While at his previous company, he noticed many Gong fans raving about the brand on LinkedIn. A couple of years later, he joined Gong's marketing team and had a blast creating an audio reel[4] of "wow" reactions from customer calls to share that enthusiasm with potential buyers. "We had so many to choose from; it was just a matter of picking the best ones," he said. After seeing the impactful audio reel Jonathan created, other companies were inspired to create their own, and you can too!

When a company genuinely focuses on creating raving fans, marketing can bypass the typical arm-twisting required to persuade customers to share their experiences—whether at industry events, in marketing materials, or on reference calls.

This magic doesn't happen because marketing *claims* there are raving fans; it happens because those fans truly exist and enjoy

---

[4] "Gong Raises $200M Series D at a $2.2B Valuation," YouTube, January 28, 2021, https://www.youtube.com/watch?v=Mi547vW3P5U.

every part of their brand experience: using the product, getting help on a technical issue, and attending a company event.

The takeaway is clear: marketing can't succeed if it approaches brand-building as a disjointed exercise, separate from the rest of the company. To create a credible brand, the entire organization must be aligned and committed. From the CEO and executive team to every business function—including recruiting coordinators, tech support engineers, and product designers—everyone plays a role. Only then can marketing serve as the steward of the brand, externalizing the company's culture and how it does business.

We'll explore employee activation in more detail later, but it's worth emphasizing its importance here. Developing operating principles that employees are proud to uphold inspires them to share their successes and experiences—on social media, with customers, and with friends who might become future employees or customers. This amplifies your reach well beyond what your budget alone could achieve. Companies like Lavender, Drift, Cribl, and Gong exemplify how strong cultures of employee activation can significantly grow a brand.

When marketing thrives as the steward of the brand ("party host") rather than its sole creator ("club owner"), you have a solid foundation for building your company's reputation. Now let's explore the tools and techniques that influence how your business is perceived.

What Kind of Human Would Your Brand Be?

Imagine a fun, trustworthy person. Someone helpful who gives you good advice along with a good laugh and is always rooting for you. They speak clearly on topics you care about and occasionally throw in a harmless curse word to make a point. You probably want to hang out with them often, right? That's how we imagined Gong would act if it were a human.

Working on our brand personality was one of the most rewarding times of my CMO chapter at Gong. The key here is to be intentional. If you don't know what you stand for, someone else will decide for you and you might not like it. There are several ways to conduct this exercise, and I'd encourage any company going through this process to hire a facilitator or agency experienced in it, as it's well worth the long-term investment.

A breakthrough moment in our process was when we decided to let two seemingly contradictory personality traits coexist within our brand: mature and friendly. Ask any startup what they want to be perceived as, and 99% will say some version of "thought leader," "trustworthy," or "mature." This makes perfect sense.

But here is where many brands get it wrong: to be perceived as trustworthy and credible, most brands follow the examples of antiquated brands that are considered authorities in their field. They neglect to realize that the authority of a large IT company or bank comes from its long-standing status in the market. It's not from the boring, safe style of writing or stock photography their corporate communications and legal teams force upon them.

Apple's early campaigns were edgy and revolutionary, compared to its recent brand. To be sure, it's still one of the world's strongest brands, but it seems to have lost some of its daring edge since its inception. The dystopian 1984 Super Bowl commercial[5]

---

[5] "1984 Apple's First Macintosh Commercial," YouTube, December 12, 2005, https://youtu.be/OYecfV3ubP8?si=L8w4PxdB3OYhb9l3.

introducing the first Macintosh and the inspiring "Think Different" commercial[6] that marked Steve Jobs' return to Apple are considered, to this day, landmark brand campaigns.

Taking inspiration from other brands can be helpful but needs to be done thoughtfully. "Many marketers think, 'can't we just copy that brand?'" said Anthony Kennada, who helped build brands like Gainsight and Hoppin. Without understanding context, timing, and audience differences, and without tweaking and personalizing it to your audience's needs, copying other brands' work will feel inauthentic.

If you're forced to read a leading analyst's report on your field, you don't have much choice but to plow through the long-winded pages in hopes of finding an interesting nugget or two. But if you're a young, unknown startup, you don't have a captive audience like the analyst firm does. You haven't yet earned the privilege of producing boring content and being unapproachable. In fact, I would argue your only chance of surviving and growing is to become as approachable and personable as you can.

"Bold, optimistic, and practical with a wink." Those were the personality traits Carilu Dietrich worked on at Atlassian. "Brand personality is often a reflection of the founder's personality. In its early days, Slack was also exceptional at incorporating some of its internal humor into the external brand. Oracle was different because the founder was data-driven and drier. That came through in the brand."

---

[6] "Apple - Think Different - Full Version," YouTube, September 30, 2013, https://www.youtube.com/watch?v=5sMBhDv4sik.

During Gong's early days, we married the standard "mature" trait with "friendly," which manifested a fun, approachable, and whimsical personality. This was virtually unheard of among B2B brands in 2018 and became a key part of our brand's success. Many of the anecdotes shared in this book tie back to this decision to establish the most authoritative brand in our space while being perceived more as a helpful friend than as a condescending corporation.

This graphic from Atreo, the Technology Marketing Agency, shows the main brand personality decisions we made in 2018.

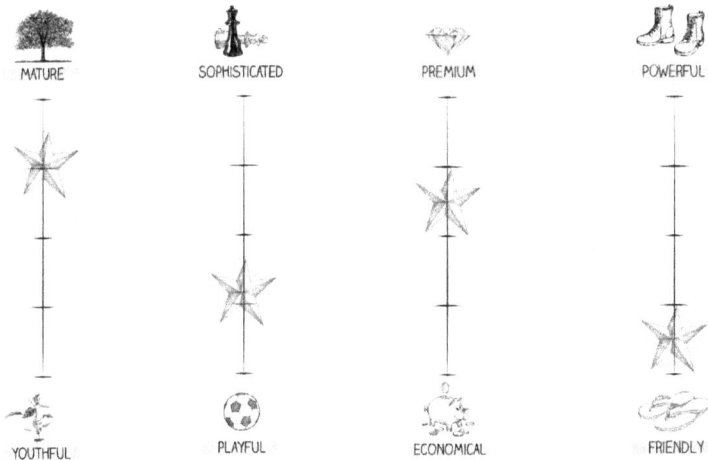

| MATURE | SOPHISTICATED | PREMIUM | POWERFUL |
| YOUTHFUL | PLAYFUL | ECONOMICAL | FRIENDLY |

This unlikely amalgamation of personality traits carried through all of our marketing campaigns and programs—from the bright colors on our website to bubble machines at event booths alongside selfie stations with Bruno, our wacky bulldog mascot. Every social media post and every customer email received meticulous care and attention to ensure it demonstrated our bubbly personality and encouraged our audience to engage with us.

Consumer-brand marketers have been acting this way for years. Can you imagine having to complete a 15-field form to view the product specs of your favorite sneaker? Probably not. So why do most B2B companies still ask their prospects to jump through fire hoops like lengthy forms and unnecessarily gated content about their own products?

Even companies selling "boring" products like insurance have realized the easiest way to our hearts, minds, and wallets is by using humor, talking lizards, and lighthearted Super Bowl commercials. Nobody wants to think about that impending earthquake or flood. We just want peace of mind served in a fun, easily digestible package.

Brands like Amazon have spoiled us and changed our expectations of businesses. If they can deliver a package overnight, why does it take your team two or three days to get back to a website inquiry? When looking for inspiration for your B2B brand or marketing campaign, you'll often find that the best, most engaging ideas come from our peers in B2C.

Intentionally give your brand a personality your audience enjoys hanging out with. Then use it to make decisions on your visual identity, tone of voice, and all brand touchpoints with your audience.

Moments of Delight

Some brand-building comes from monumental efforts like launching a new website, putting on a large-scale customer event, or planning an epic Super Bowl commercial. But most of the time, brands gain momentum through small, everyday interactions, like a routine email.

If you've ever used a software product, you know most companies send out their updated privacy policy around January or February. It's a yawn-inducing practice most companies invest little thought in. When my team at Gong had to send out our annual notice, they asked me for guidance.

"Don't make it boring," I said.

They delivered big time by seizing this opportunity to delight our customers and add another layer of "raving fandom" to our brand. It started with a startling subject line:

"Our lawyers made us do this."

Inside the email, they found our usual lighthearted tone:

> Privacy. Protection. Personal Data.
>
> This is likely the umpteenth email you've received in the past few months that has referenced one (or more) of those 3 words and phrases.
>
> We didn't want to miss out on any of the fun, so we went ahead and also updated our Privacy Policy to reflect the new requirements of the California Consumer Privacy Act (CCPA).
>
> As it turns out, we are also required by law to update our policy AND to tell you that we are updating our policy.
>
> ✅ and ✅.

We even threw in a "Mission Accomplished" Britney Spears meme for good measure[7].

This image shows the privacy policy email we sent out. Ms. Spears' face has been obfuscated here for copyright reasons.

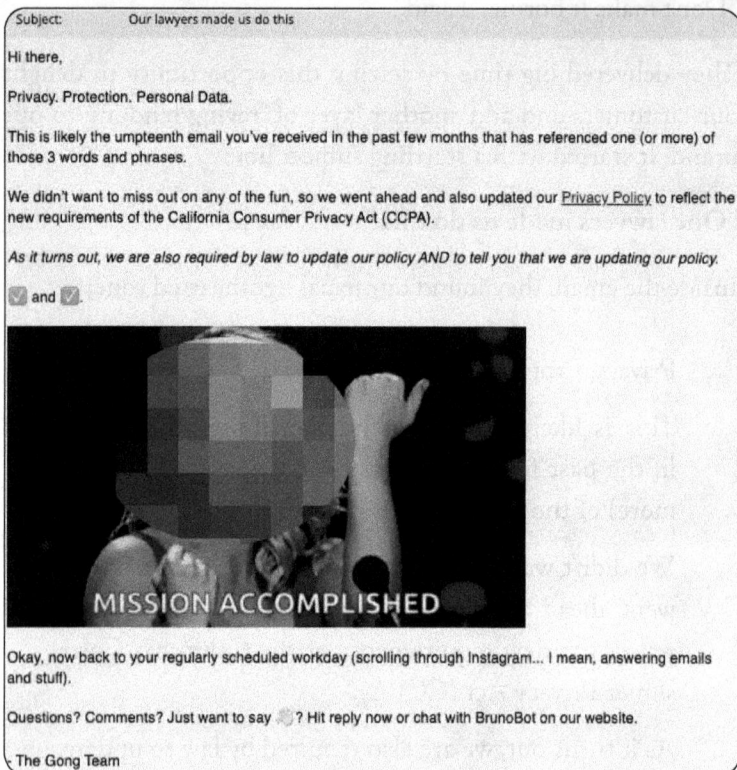

> **Subject:**   Our lawyers made us do this
>
> Hi there,
>
> Privacy. Protection. Personal Data.
>
> This is likely the umpteenth email you've received in the past few months that has referenced one (or more) of those 3 words and phrases.
>
> We didn't want to miss out on any of the fun, so we went ahead and also updated our Privacy Policy to reflect the new requirements of the California Consumer Privacy Act (CCPA).
>
> *As it turns out, we are also required by law to update our policy AND to tell you that we are updating our policy.*
>
> ✅ and ✅.
>
> MISSION ACCOMPLISHED
>
> Okay, now back to your regularly scheduled workday (scrolling through Instagram... I mean, answering emails and stuff).
>
> Questions? Comments? Just want to say 👋? Hit reply now or chat with BrunoBot on our website.
>
> - The Gong Team

---

7 Udi Ledergor, "39.5% Email Open Rate. after Our Privacy Policy Email Exploded ...," February 17, 2020, https://www.linkedin.com/posts/udiledergor_395-email-open-rate-after-our-privacy-activity-6635244378006913024-j2fi?utm_source=share&utm_medium=member_desktop.

Our email saw a whopping 39.5% open rate, roughly double the industry standard[8]. But its success in elevating our brand didn't stop there: it went viral and got posted on Twitter (now X), LinkedIn, and Medium[9], as customers shared their excitement about a potentially boring email actually being funny and entertaining.

Generating Word of Mouth

Many CEOs I advise complain to me about their marketing content collecting cobwebs while nobody engages with it. When I look at their content, I inevitably find it to be self-serving, dealing with their company's products, features, and awards.

"When was the last time you shared content like this from a company you didn't work for?" I challenge them.

"Never," they reply as the penny drops.

Seth Godin coined the term "purple cow" in its namesake book to explain the idea that companies must build things worth noticing, products or ideas that are truly unique; otherwise, they won't sell. If you're driving on a countryside road and see a black-and-white cow, Godin explains, you won't think twice about it. But if you see a purple cow, you'll pull out your phone, snap a photo, and send it to your friends. That's the type of moment every marketer hopes to create.

We'll take a deep dive into content creation and distribution later, but it's worth mentioning here that a great way to grow

---

[8] "Email Marketing Benchmarks & Industry Statistics," Mailchimp.com, accessed January 24, 2025, https://mailchimp.com/resources/email-marketing-benchmarks/.
[9] Negin Safdari, "Why Did Gong.Io's Consumer Privacy Email Go Viral?," Medium, March 19, 2020, https://medium.com/the-helm/the-recipe-to-creating-viral-emails-941a8c23ca8f.

your brand is by creating "purple cow" moments your customers and prospects find so exciting they're compelled to share them with colleagues. Sending a thoughtful gift goes a long way. Thankful customers are likely to share the kind gesture on social media, earning you many new fans.

Another great way of getting your audience to share something is to make them feel part of a secret community or club. Gong caters mostly to sales professionals, so when we post a sales-related meme, especially at a sensitive time like the last day of the quarter, it's likely that thousands of our followers will appreciate the moment of levity in an otherwise stressful day and share it with their networks, signaling they feel seen.[10]

The diversity of these examples demonstrates that *everything* is marketing. Your brand is built through thousands of moments and touchpoints. The best way of intentionally creating a brand is to get the entire company behind it and then have marketing act as a steward of the brand, amplifying reality instead of creating a facade. Embodying the personality of an approachable, fun, and interesting human being will delight your customers and generate word of mouth, an incredibly effective marketing channel.

Company brands are important, but they can't exist in a vacuum. As they gain recognition, the market groups companies into categories. Bold companies choose to create and lead a category while other successful companies expand or disrupt their categories. Which brings us to the question our next chapter will answer: should you build a category?

---

[10] Gong, "I'm Fine, Everything's Fine," April 10, 2023, https://www.linkedin.com/posts/gong-io_im-fine-everythings-fine-activity-7051297833819258880-mNey/.

CHAPTER 5

SHOULD YOU BUILD A CATEGORY?

"If I ever write a sequel, I'll title it:
<u>Don't Create a Category</u>."

—Anthony Kennada, Author of *Category Creation*

"Dear God, send me a line," prayed an exhausted Frances Gerety before getting into bed one night in 1947. She then scribbled something on a piece of paper and went to sleep. When she woke up in the morning, she found that she had written:

"A diamond is forever."

Gerety was a young copywriter at the Philadelphia advertising agency N.W. Ayer & Son, working on a new campaign for the diamond conglomerate De Beers. She went on to write all the diamond company's ads for 25 years. In 1999, two weeks before her death at the age of 83, Advertising Age named it the slogan of the century.[11]

---

[11] J. Courtney Sullivan, "How Diamonds Became Forever," The New York Times, May 3, 2013, https://www.nytimes.com/2013/05/05/fashion/weddings/how-americans-learned-to-love-diamonds.html.

While there is no shortage of great category-creation stories, such as Uber creating ride shares, Hubspot inventing inbound marketing, and Salesforce pioneering the age of cloud computing, I find the story of De Beers[12] to be particularly enchanting, for its almost sinister cleverness.

Spoiler alert: diamonds aren't nearly as rare as you might think. Since the discovery of vast diamond mines in Africa in 1870, there has never been a real shortage of diamonds in the world. In fact, De Beers had the opposite problem. The company was sitting on such a large stockpile of diamonds that it feared their market price could plummet unless it did something to dramatically increase their demand.

Diamonds being a symbol of love and commitment is a fairly recent idea. On the eve of World War II, only 10% of engagement rings contained diamonds.[13] De Beers hired N.W. Ayer & Son to create a marketing campaign that would appeal to consumers' emotions, as diamonds have little intrinsic value. How successful were they? By the end of the 20th century, 80% of engagement rings shimmered with diamonds.

One of several brilliant components of the De Beers campaign was loaning diamond jewelry to celebrities for red-carpet events, a tradition that continues to this day, and then filling the newspapers' gossip columns with sightings of celebrities wearing them.

---

[12] Edward Jay Epstein, "Have You Ever Tried to Sell a Diamond?," The Atlantic, February 7, 2024, https://www.theatlantic.com/magazine/archive/1982/02/have-you-ever-tried-to-sell-a-diamond/304575/.

[13] Laurence Cawley, "De Beers Myth: Do People Spend a Month's Salary on a Diamond Engagement Ring?," BBC News, May 16, 2014, https://www.bbc.com/news/magazine-27371208.

Another intriguing component was born from a legal limitation imposed on the company. Because they controlled global supply, sourcing an estimated 80% of the world's rough diamonds at the time, antitrust laws prohibited the company from directly doing business in the United States. They created other legal entities to circumvent this restriction and their ads could not directly promote De Beers, so the agency had to get very creative.

This is where category-creation magic came into play: by creating understated ads that simply said, "A diamond is forever," without mentioning any brand name, consumers were caught off guard. It was easy to believe you were reading a public service announcement. Later ads contained detailed buying guides on what to look for in a diamond and how much to spend on an engagement ring—now you know who invented the unsettling "two months' salary" rule.

What these ads ultimately did was promote *the category* of diamonds as eternal symbols of love and commitment, changing the buying habits of grooms-to-be for almost a century to come. De Beers realized it was easier to drive agreement on a common "need" (commemorating important life moments) than to force-sell their own product. All they had to do was convince people to buy diamonds—any diamonds. Eight of ten diamonds would come from De Beers, so they didn't worry about not promoting their brand name.

Category Design

Categories are created when a critical mass of buyers decides it can no longer live without a certain product group, it then goes mainstream, and a category is born. But market players can accelerate its creation and affect the shaping of the nascent category. That's where category design comes in: Apple made touch-screens the standard for smartphones and Salesforce made Software-as-a-Service (SaaS) the common way to run business software.

Play Bigger, an agency that helps companies create and lead new market categories, describes category design as a business strategy that focuses on creating a new marketing category, which can then be monetized and monopolized before competitors can enter the space. The underlying idea is that by establishing a new niche that is free of competition, your company has an excellent chance of dominating it.[14]

Sounds great, but is it right for *you?*

Why You Shouldn't Build a Category

Category creation isn't for the faint of heart. There are good reasons for not building a category and great alternatives to consider before embarking on a risky category-creation journey. The main reasons for reconsidering category creation are:

- There's probably a better way to win.
- The cost of market education.
- The risk of getting it wrong.

Each of these should give you pause and warrants special consideration. Let's dive into each of them.

---

[14] "What Is Category Design?," Play Bigger, accessed January 24, 2025, https://www.playbigger.com/categorydesign.

There's probably a better way to win. Before launching a costly category-creation project, stop and consider your alternatives. The vast majority of successful companies did not *create* a category around themselves. Perhaps they *redefined* their category to extend or disrupt it.

Finding an underserved market in an existing space is another great way to go—Hubspot did this for small businesses who needed a CRM solution but couldn't find one built for their business size.

Specializing in one industry or market is another smart choice— if you localize a global product category to the needs and language of, say, Flemish speakers in Belgium, you could become a leader in that market. The same idea applies to specializing in an industry, like creating an email marketing platform for oil and gas companies. Or carving out an overlooked component within a product category and expanding it to a stand-alone solution so good that companies would buy it on top of their existing solution.

The point is that there are many ways of winning within an existing category, without carrying the heavy burden of fabricating a new one.

The cost of market education. Educating even a small market segment on the problem you solve, the realm of possible solutions, and why your category-in-the-making is the best solution to their problem is a monumental effort requiring considerable talent, energy, funds, and patience.

Categories are created over years, not months or fiscal quarters. Underestimating the time and effort involved in building your category will set you up for certain failure. Everyone— from the board of directors to the CEO to each and every employee—should understand your company is setting out on a category-creation journey, which will take years to complete.

Milestones and leading indicators should be set for the short term, but nobody should expect a new category to exist within six months. After all, you're trying to uproot old working habits of an entire market and create new, better ones. Crucially, markets (*buyers* of your product and its competitors) create the category—not companies like yours, trying to *sell* products.

We are all programmed to resist change. It's in our DNA. So there's no reason to expect the nature of the beast to change just because you need to urgently create a new category to help sell your product.

The risk of getting it wrong. You could get any strategic motion wrong, but working on the wrong category is an extremely painful decision to err on. Spending years of effort and millions of dollars on educating the market on "your way," only to realize the market has drifted another way, could put your company at existential risk.

Imagine aligning your entire company—product development and go-to-market teams—on where you think the market is going. But the majority of customers, analysts, and other stakeholders ultimately adopt a different vision, perhaps seeded by one of your competitors.

That's exactly what happened to Google with its Glass smart glasses. The same happened to Juicero[15], who tried to reinvent

---

[15] Sam Levin, "Squeezed Out: Widely Mocked Startup Juicero Is Shutting Down," The Guardian, September 1, 2017, https://www.theguardian.com/technology/2017/sep/01/juicero-silicon-valley-shutting-down.

the way we make juices at home. Huge risk is inevitable when embarking on a journey like this, so it's important to recognize it upfront and agree it's worth taking for the potential upside.

Google easily survived because Glass was a single product in its large portfolio. Juicero was not as lucky and shut down when its single big bet failed.

Drift started with a simple website chatbot categorized as conversational marketing. When Tricia Gellman joined the company as CMO, she saw an opportunity to create a bigger category. "We provided more value than other players in our category. By calling it 'conversational *revenue*' we could talk with revenue leaders, not just marketers, and raise our prices. But no other companies caught up with our category narrative and Drift's founders were not totally bought in, either," she explained. The company eventually retracted the new category idea. If other companies and analysts don't join your movement, you don't have a category.

Any way you look at it, the road to building a new category is riddled with pitfalls. Consider the less risky and cheaper alternatives first, before deciding category-building is the best solution for you.

Why You Should Build a Category

So you considered the alternatives and you want to build a category. Understanding the benefits of category ownership will help you make the right decision and advocate the big move within your company. The biggest benefits include:

- Creating a new budget line item.
- Defining the category narrative.

- Commanding a premium price.
- Earning a higher valuation.

One or more of these reasons could be your justification for building a new category. Let's explore them in detail.

Creating a new budget line item. If you're trying to sell a product or service and most of your prospects don't yet have a budget line item for what you're selling, category-building might be your best move. If you're successful, you'll end up in a market with a budget line item dedicated to your category, making it considerably easier to sell your product.

It's much harder to sell when you have to educate your buyer on the problem you solve, help them win their internal fight over budget, and then convince them your solution is the best alternative. Having a budget line item shortcuts most of that process and allows you to skip to demonstrating how your solution is better than others.

Defining the category narrative. This is the broader purpose and aspiration to advance an industry. As Anthony Kennada writes in his book, *Category Creation*, industry analysts don't create categories. They report on them once the market has created them and made the product a must-have.

Analyst coverage is a *lagging* indicator of category-building success. The defining companies affect analysts' perceptions by carefully planting seeds for the category narrative.

If you're successful, analysts end up describing your category in *your* own terms. That's a great measure of your efforts' success.

Commanding a premium price. Buyers often pay more for leading brands. This is true for consumer products—Tesla charges premium prices for its electric cars compared to lesser-known brands. It's equally true for B2B products—Gainsight charged premium prices for its customer success software and Qualtrics did the same with its customer experience software.

A leading brand name carries the promise of having a reliable product and a sustainable company, which will support its customers for years to come. In many cases, this trust earns companies the right to charge premium prices.

A fatal mistake some brands make is trying to convince their buyers that this axiom of market leaders charging premium prices isn't true in *their* space. They claim their brand is both the highest quality *and* the lowest in price, which markets find very difficult to swallow. This can lead to a brand losing both its credibility and its market share, as confused customers shift to other brands with a clearer value proposition.

You are either the best in your space and charge accordingly, or you're the cheapest, which is a valid positioning, but requires a supporting claim along the lines of, "We sell 80% of the leading brand's features at 50% of the price." If you had 100% of the leading brand's features, you'd be selling at premium prices your market would be willing to pay.

Earning a higher valuation. Look at the public stock markets and you'll find that category-creators are often valued at premiums compared to secondary players in their categories. Being a category king means you're more innovative than other companies, have the resources and skills to pull off such an ambitious endeavor, and—at least for a while—you get to be the leader.

All this evokes investor trust, which translates to valuation premiums. The old adage, "the winner takes all," turns out to be remarkably accurate in B2B categories, where the winner takes *most.*

"Category kings" often dominate 76%[16] of their markets' revenue share and continue holding the lion's share even when their share shrinks as other players catch up and disrupt the category dynamics.

These combined benefits make a compelling case for building a category, but make sure you've first considered the alternatives and that you have the long-term resources and internal buy-in to pull off the ambitious endeavor.

Creating the Revenue Intelligence Category

In 2016, Gong launched its first product for sales teams. It recorded, transcribed, and analyzed their customer conversations to help them pinpoint coaching moments and opportunities for improving their outcomes. We needed to quickly describe to the market what we did in simple terms.

A couple of other companies had similar products and used "conversation intelligence" to describe them, so we latched onto that category as a start. The conversation intelligence category

---

[16] Lucy Vigrass, "How Unicorns Grow," Harvard Business Review, December 17, 2020, https://hbr.org/2016/01/how-unicorns-grow.

served us well for three years, during which we experienced exponential growth.

In early 2019, we realized we had two serious problems we needed to solve. We suspected that breaking away from conversation intelligence, in favor of a new category we'd build, would help solve those problems.

The first problem was differentiating from our competitors whose vision was shortsighted and narrower than ours. They described conversation intelligence as being mostly about recording sales calls, searching for keywords in the transcripts, and listening to calls to find coaching opportunities.

At the same time, Gong envisioned the future of our product and category as including building a sales pipeline powered by artificial intelligence, smarter ways of forecasting sales results, and much more. Whenever we tried "selling" this vision to customers, we came across a common objection from buyers comparing us to competitors with a much smaller product and vision and a fittingly lower price.

The second problem we were looking to solve was that the typical buyer of our product, the Chief Revenue Officer (CRO), would often hear us describe what we do as conversation intelligence and immediately delegate the next call with us to someone more junior in their organization, such as a member of the sales enablement team, which typically deals "with tools like yours."

We took a bet on a new category name, which would allow us to better differentiate ourselves against the competition *and* keep the attention of senior sales leaders for longer. We knew this initiative had a much higher likelihood of succeeding if a smart person was dedicated to running it. At the time, we were interviewing several candidates for a product marketing role at Gong. One of those candidates was Sheena Badani, a Harvard Business School M.B.A. with several years of marketing experience, who impressed us during her interviews to the point that we agreed she should lead our category-creation efforts.

Hiring Sheena was crucial to keeping our attention on the process and making sure at least one person lived and breathed this effort every day without getting distracted by other initiatives. I'm not aware of other companies that have put this level of dedicated category-creation effort in place.

Sheena expertly facilitated an intense few months of internal workshops, as we considered different category names for our vision of the market, eventually landing on "revenue intelligence." We believed "intelligence" created continuity with our previous category name while "revenue" elevated our status compared to "conversation," capturing more interest from senior sales leaders. Lastly, having a new category name would help us differentiate ourselves from the old category and represent the wave of the future.

To give ourselves the best chance of succeeding in this risky endeavor, our marketing efforts took a new approach for the following three years: Instead of focusing on promoting the Gong brand, we shifted to focusing on why revenue intelligence was better than other approaches to building high-performing revenue teams.

The counterintuitive move shifted attention away from the company and onto the new category. We led with a category slogan,

"Goodbye Opinions, Hello Reality," suggesting that sales leaders making strategic decisions should stop trusting hunches and unsubstantiated opinions and look at data-backed reality instead. This was crucial to getting market players to buy into the idea.

Turns out, it's a lot easier to get a large number of people to agree on a common problem and broad solution than to convince them to buy a specific product. Hubspot did this when it evangelized "inbound marketing" and Gainsight did it with "customer success."

Next, we set up a "lightning-strike moment" on the category launch date. We hosted an event for customers and prospects and named it "Celebrate: The Revenue Intelligence Summit," alluding to it covering the whole category rather than just our company.

We even gave the event's website and venue a unique visual treatment—colors, typography, and imagery—to set it apart from our company brand and make it appear as if this was an event bigger than what we'd throw for our customers.

As the crowd settled in the SFJAZZ Center, lights painted the stage with our brand's shade of purple. Amit Bendov, Gong's CEO, walked on stage as I advanced his presentation slides from the control booth.

He described the problems revenue leaders were facing, not knowing what was happening on their customer calls. As he described this state of "haziness," a fog machine filled the stage with cloud-like smoke, which nearly got us into trouble with the local fire department.

At the climactic moment of his keynote, angelic sounds immersed the audience as Amit revealed our new category, "... we're calling it: Revenue Intelligence!"

We milked everything we could from that moment by releasing a press announcement[17] exactly as our CEO named the new category on stage. Knowing that Dreamforce, the largest software conference in town, was taking place in San Francisco the following month, we did a full station takeover of the Montgomery BART station, featuring our category slogan, "Goodbye Opinions, Hello Reality" in four languages. We even wrapped 20 rideshare cars with it and had them swarm around Moscone Center, where thousands of sales professionals attending Dreamforce could get a ride to and from the conference.

We kept the momentum going by launching *Reveal: The Revenue Intelligence Podcast*. As we did with our conference, we chose to "own" the entire category with the name of the podcast instead of calling it *The Gong Podcast*, creating the perception of a big category forming around us. "We were targeting Chief Revenue Officers, who get a lot of their information from listening to podcasts," said Sheena Badani, who led Gong's category-creation efforts. "So we came up with the podcast, which took off and became a hit with CROs." This turned out to be a great experiment while staying close to our customers to understand what channels and formats work best for them.

Thanks to the great preparation work done by the entire marketing team at Gong, the moment we flipped the switch on our

[17] Gong, "Gong Charts New Future for Sales Leaders, Launches Revenue Intelligence," PR Newswire, October 8, 2019, https://www.prnewswire.com/news-releases/gong-charts-new-future-for-sales-leaders-launches-revenue-intelligence-300933657.html.

new category name, our website instantly updated and all customer-facing sales materials were upgraded to showcase our new category name.

We ran internal training sessions to ensure every employee could speak confidently about the new category, why it's the way of the future, and how it's superior to the "legacy" conversation intelligence category.

We even launched a "Revenue Intelligence Maturity Assessment" on our website, where interested companies could assess their level of maturity on our new scale, giving the impression it's crucial to succeeding as a revenue organization.

Gong had been known for several years for publishing valuable, data-backed research on topics that sales professionals cared about. We quickly reframed old content and authored new content, like interviews with sales leaders using revenue intelligence to build a better team, which positioned Gong as the leader of the emerging category.

We used customer stories as social proof to create credibility in the market for the nascent category and an element of FOMO among those not yet using it. With our customers' permission, we reworked some older customer stories to strategically insert "revenue intelligence" in them and ensure that from that point on, all new customer stories explicitly used our new language.

At the same time, we scheduled multiple press and analyst briefings. By feeding the press with customer stories, where the prepared customers used "revenue intelligence" language, reporters found it easy to quote them verbatim. Industry analysts, who consult enterprise customers on software purchases, started buying into our vision and category framing.

All these efforts had one thing in common: they were aimed at propelling the revenue intelligence category instead of focusing on our company. This marketing motion required confidence and discipline in the face of internal objections like, "But our logo is too small!" or "How will they know this is a Gong ad?"

These efforts continued for almost three years before we could confidently say they were bearing fruit and revenue intelligence had become a sustainable category, with which analyst firms, competitors, and customers had aligned.

How did we measure our success and know we had made it?

Measuring Category Success

Measuring category creation is not an exact science, so you'll have to get comfortable with not being able to measure every single aspect with precision. Having said that, there are quite a few proxies you can use for measuring your progress on category creation and leadership. These are some of the most useful metrics my team and I used.

Google searches. On the day before our category announcement, we measured precisely zero Google searches for "revenue intelligence." We monitored this number every month and saw healthy growth in monthly searches. If nobody's searching for your category name, they either don't see a need for it or they don't know about it yet. In either case, you'll want to know.

Podcast downloads. The revenue intelligence podcast started, as all podcasts do, with zero downloads. We tracked our downloads every week and celebrated when we achieved 100,000 within a year or so and then 200,000 downloads at the end of its second year. These milestones indicated our category content was resonating with our audience.

Email subscribers and social followers. The more subscribers and followers you amass, the more you know your category messaging is resonating with the market. Within a relatively short time, Gong's LinkedIn following grew to 250,000+ and we enjoyed hundreds of thousands of email subscribers eager to find our content in their inbox.

Event attendees. More often than not, we frame our events' agenda around category content instead of self-promotion. Growing event registration and attendance are great signs of your message cutting through the noise and resonating with buyers.

Analyst reports. Industry analysts and review sites like Gartner, Forrester, and G2 each have their own requirements for reporting on a new category. Typically, they like to see 10–12 vendors, a healthy number of customers, and meaningful revenue before they report on a category. G2 tends to move faster than the others, while Gartner can take several years before creating a meaningful report on a new category. In my experience, Forrester lies somewhere in the middle.

Educate the relevant analysts in your space early and often. Run strategy days with them to get their feedback on your vision for the category. Inquire about what they are seeing with other players in your market and ask for suggestions on gaps they see in your product offering and roadmap.

Obviously, you don't have to take all of their advice because sometimes they won't "get it" the way you do, but you should listen carefully nonetheless as these analysts are talking to your buyers and sharing how they see your category and your company's strengths and weaknesses.

Once you and other players gain enough traction, you can expect to see reports being published by relevant analysts. This is a fantastic measure of your category shifting from a vision and a dream into a tangible product category the market has validated.

It took roughly two years from our category launch to see the first Forrester and Gartner reports on our space, positioning Gong as a clear leader. G2 moved faster, as it often does. Make sure you have the patience to wait this long (or longer) and don't give up on the analysts. The player who spends the most time with them will likely have the most impact on the category narrative the analysts include in their reports and guidance to buyers.

Media coverage. Every time a reputable publication writes a story about your space, you can count it as a point toward your category-design efforts. Note I'm referring to *earned* media, not *paid* media. Counting paid placements would be cheating yourself because you're trying to measure external validation of your category, not your own promotion of it.

Competitor shifts. Within weeks of launching our new category, we noticed several copycat players, who had been following our every move, updated their website and marketing materials to reflect our new category language. That was an amazing validation of our messaging landing and of our leadership of the space. The more players use the same type of language, the faster the category is created in the eyes of the market, the analysts, and the press.

Win rate vs. status quo. Most companies lose most of their sales opportunities not to a direct competitor, but to the status quo, otherwise known as "no decision." One reason this happens is an underdeveloped category. The need for a product in your category hasn't been fully established, so many buyers simply don't have a budget line item for it yet.

Once your category gains momentum, you can expect it to show up in your win rate against the status quo: you should be winning more deals as fewer deals end up with "no decision." Note there are other intervening factors like an economic downturn that might mess with these numbers, so take them with a grain of salt, but look into them for clues of your category strength. Pro tip: revenue intelligence software like Gong's can greatly simplify conducting this win-loss analysis.

Market share. If you have access to sales numbers or the number of customers your competitors have, you can start building a market share map to understand your share within the category. Note this is a measure of your leadership within your category more than it is of the category's maturity. To estimate the category growth, look at the growing size of the entire sales pie, including all players.

Customers using category language. Measure the percentage of customer calls where your category language is used. You can expect to see this trending up and to the right as your category messaging repeatedly meets your customers in marketing materials, on sales calls, and at events. Once again, revenue intelligence software is the easiest way to accomplish this.

Measuring all these metrics can be exhausting and perhaps you only need a subset of them. The point is you're not in the dark when it comes to measuring your category-creation efforts. So pick the metrics that work for you and bask in the glory of your successful efforts.

Building a category is not for everyone. There are safer and cheaper alternatives you should seriously consider. But creating a sustainable category has a huge positive impact on a company's long-term viability. Pick a simple story for your category narrative, one you won't get tired of repeating thousands of times to analysts, customers, and partners—because you'll have to. Choose the right metrics to measure your efforts and bam, you're off to the races!

Whether you design a new category or expand an existing one, you'll have to get really good at content marketing, a surprisingly effective growth technique, and the topic of our next chapter.

CHAPTER 6

WOULD YOU PAY FOR YOUR CONTENT?

"The opposite of courage is not cowardice, it is conformity. Even a dead fish can go with the flow."

—Jim Hightower

"No fucking way!"

Benjamin's comment was one of thousands that Gong received in response to the article we posted on LinkedIn. Our research suggested that salespeople shouldn't avoid swearing on sales calls. We found the most effective use of the technique is mirroring your prospect's swearing. You will achieve a small uptick in win rates by swearing first, but for maximum effect, wait until your prospect signals they appreciate this conversation style by using it first.

Nothing prepared us for the response this content piece received. *Fast Company*, the widely-followed news site, ran a story[18] covering highlights of our research. Within hours of publication, a Canadian radio station called to interview me on air about it.

---

[18] Udi Ledergor, "Here Is Why You Should Swear at Work, According to Science," Fast Company, December 15, 2019, https://www.fastcompany.com/90442773/here-is-why-you-should-swear-at-work-according-to-science.

Thousands of sales professionals commented on, reacted to, and shared our research.

Reactions fell in two buckets: those like Benjamin, relieved with the permission we gave them, frantically tagging their bosses or co-workers—and others clearly appalled at our suggestion.

It was a marketer's dream come true.

The best way I've found to grow brand awareness and demand generation for a B2B startup is through content marketing. So it's surprising how bad most companies are at it.

Marketing is simultaneously playing two games, the short game and the long game. The short game is with prospects currently in the market for a solution like yours. The long game is with those not currently in the market for your solution and is a totally different game. But how do you know which game you're playing with whom? Enter the 95-5 rule.

The 95-5 Rule

Professor John Dawes of the B2B Institute, a LinkedIn think tank researching new approaches to B2B growth, summarized his report, *Advertising effectiveness and the 95-5 rule: most B2B buyers are not in the market right now*[19]:

> "It might surprise you to learn that up to 95% of business clients are not in the market for many goods and

---

[19] Professor John Dawes, *Advertising effectiveness and the 95-5 rule: most B2B buyers are not in the market right now,* The B2B Institute, accessed January 25, 2025, https://assets.foleon.com/eu-central-1/de-uploads-7e3kk3/30230/advertising-effectiveness-and-the-95-5-rule_002.87e3217ac41e.pdf.

services at any one time. This is a deceptively simple fact, but it has a profound implication for advertising. It means that advertising mostly hits B2B buyers who aren't going to buy anytime soon. In turn, that tells us about how advertising works: it mainly works by building and refreshing memory links to the brand. These memory links activate when buyers do come into the market. So, if your advertising is better at building brand-relevant memories, your brand becomes more competitive. The question to ask is: 'Does our advertising do that?'"

To illustrate that academic speak, let's say you're selling home storage solutions. Most people buy those only once in a while. To keep them engaged with your brand while they're not actively buying, you could send weekly tips on home improvement, including how to keep things tidy and organized.

Those tips would create a memory link between your brand and organizing and keeping your home tidy. When your prospect is finally fed up with having too much stuff and not enough space, what will be the first brand they think of as they look to buy a storage solution? Yours!

Because you've been feeding them with valuable content that keeps your brand top of mind for them on all things storage, when the buying moment arrives, those memory links activate and your name pops up when they need it most.

Here's how the 95-5 rule works in B2B: businesses tend to replace major equipment and software once every five years or so. That means if they just purchased, say, a new CRM system, they're typically not in the market for another one for the next five years. Hence, only 20% of relevant companies are in the market for a new CRM system this year, which translates to 5% of them being in the market in any given calendar quarter.

Now, here's the rub—most marketers tend to focus on sales-oriented marketing and advertising, which usually talks about their product, its features, special terms for buying it today, etc. They do this because they're under pressure to bring qualified buyers to the table. Those efforts might be effective on the 5% of companies in the market today. But the other 95% will quickly tune out, unsubscribe from your sales emails, unfollow your social media channels, and generally put you on their *Do Not Call* list, because you're offering them zero relevance and value.

Companies who excel at marketing figure out how to shine at both games: capture the existing demand from the 5% in the market *and* nurture the 95% not in the market, creating memory links that activate when they do move into the buying market.

This is easier said than done, as it requires aligning many stakeholders like the CEO, CFO, and board, on playing the long game, withholding expectations on short-term returns on those long-term marketing investments, and—perhaps most challenging—having the patience to wait for the results of these efforts to slowly bear fruit.

An extreme example of the 95-5 rule happened at Gainsight, a customer success software provider. When I spoke with Anthony Kennada, formerly the CMO at Gainsight, he said:

> "There was no 5%. Our job was to create the 95% because people didn't even understand what we were

solving for. We made a huge effort to educate the market on customer churn being 'the silent killer.' We created content on how a dedicated customer success team could solve for that. We built a community, events, and content around *the problem*. We created empathy for this new idea, tying into a larger trend and a community that validated its realness. Once you're associated with the problem, you can start solving it."

Anthony and his team understood that when you describe your customers' problems with clarity, they will associate you with the solution. Gainsight applied the 95-5 rule successfully, but Anthony cautions, "You never know whether the 5% are going to catch up with your efforts fast enough to build a lucrative business. Only in hindsight it's clear."

Marketers who misunderstand or ignore the long-term game will see limited returns on their marketing investments as only a small fraction of potential buyers respond to their sales messages. What's even worse is the reduced efficiency and long-term losses associated with 95% of their potential buyers tuning out of their marketing altogether.

Chris Orlob, who created Gong's content for three years, believes that the problem is that marketing is such a visible craft, everyone thinks they understand it. When I asked him to explain, he said, "Scroll through LinkedIn for 30 seconds and you'll find five examples of this. Some folks don't understand the buyer-journey steps and ignore the 95-5 rule, 'pitch-slapping' their audience instead of providing true value."

The best marketing teams weaponize the 95-5 rule, creating content that nurtures and engages the majority of accounts not open to sales offers, so when they're ready to buy, the first brand they think of is the one that's provided them with valuable content, not expecting them to immediately buy anything. Great content marketing is uniquely effective at engaging target buyers over time, and positions you as a thought leader in your space.

Once your prospects derive value from your content and give you permission to continue communicating with them, say, by subscribing to your email list or following you on social media, it's up to you to lead your prospects through their buying journey. The common marketing technique for doing this is a nurturing campaign, which progresses from broad-appeal content to qualified-buyer content around your product.

A good nurturing campaign is part art, part science. When executed successfully, it gracefully guides your prospects through their buying journey, empowering them to feel in control of the buying process and not as if you, the vendor, are forcing them down your sales funnel. As the old saying goes, people love buying but hate being sold to.

Great content marketing is not just effective—it's also *efficient*. Most B2B startups can allocate only a small budget to their early-days marketing efforts. When you allocate the majority of your resources to nurturing and engaging the 95% who aren't in buying mode yet, you can stretch budgets much further, using low-cost organic marketing channels like social media, email, and speaking opportunities to produce stellar results on a shoestring budget.

Every marketer dreams of creating engaging content with the least amount of resources. So how do you create and distribute great content marketing?

Let's dive in.

Content Marketing ≠ Product Marketing

Everyone understands product vendors produce content with the ultimate goal of selling their product. But not all marketers know how to create interesting, engaging content their buyers enjoy reading. Most B2B content marketing feels so salesy, you feel like showering after consuming it.

I asked Jonathan Costet, who managed growth marketing at Gong, to give me some examples. He said, "We see this everywhere. While articles listing 10 ways to solve a problem can be helpful, if the first item on the list pitches your product, you're doing it wrong. Another common mistake is inviting people to a thought-leadership webinar, which ends up being a 45-minute sales pitch." Buyers' "bullshit meters" will easily detect thinly veiled sales efforts disguised as valuable content.

Content marketing is the process of creating and distributing content, which provides value to your prospects and has little to do with your product. Our very first piece of content at Gong demonstrated this well. We analyzed 25,000 customer calls and surfaced five secrets of the perfect sales pitch.

We shared what the data told us about sales calls: how long a salesperson should talk, how many questions they should ask, and when to bring up pricing. The piece provided tremendous value to salespeople without overtly promoting our product.

At its best, content marketing uses proprietary data or analysis exclusive to your company. Great marketing can create exciting content for any industry. Are you selling web monitoring software? Surface insights from analyzing your customers' website traffic figures. Capturing surgical video footage? Analyze the data for golden nuggets like common areas where surgeons can improve. The important thing is to offer exclusive content your audience can't get elsewhere. A good formula to keep in mind is this:

$$\begin{bmatrix} \text{Your} \\ \text{prospects'} \\ \text{challenges} \end{bmatrix} + \begin{bmatrix} \text{Exclusive} \\ \text{content that} \\ \text{helps solve} \\ \text{these} \\ \text{challenges} \end{bmatrix} = \begin{bmatrix} \text{Great} \\ \text{content} \\ \text{marketing} \end{bmatrix}$$

It's OK to include a link to your company's website or a passing mention of your product if the context begs for it, but no more. Great content marketers resist temptation and don't go on rants listing off product features and case studies.

Product marketing, in contrast, is the content and process involved in taking your product to market. It includes everything from core messaging and product descriptions on your website to sales decks, product data sheets, and customer case studies. This is where you *should* go into every benefit and feature of your product, explaining not only how it is similar to other players in your category, but also what differentiates it from the rest. Now that we have a better understanding of what great content marketing *isn't*, let's break down what it *is*.

Great Content Marketing

Every piece of exceptional content I've created or consumed shares three key attributes. Beyond being interesting to the audience, it's also relevant, timely, and immediately applicable.

Relevant

Ordinary content feels generic, but extraordinary content feels tailor-made for the audience. Consider Michelin, the tire company: they realized they could sell more tires if customers drove more. So, they created the world's most famous restaurant guide to encourage people to take road trips for great meals. It worked phenomenally well. Similarly, HubSpot produced hundreds of articles, templates, and calculators to help marketers tackle daily challenges. Gong did the same for salespeople.

"We shared some counterintuitive tips in an article titled 'Selling to the C-Suite,'" recalls Chris Orlob, who created Gong's content marketing for three years. "One data point that surprised us was how win rates plummeted if you asked more than four questions during discovery. It countered the popular practice of asking as many questions as possible." At the end of the article he wrote, Chris included a call-to-action to register for a webinar on the same topic. About 3,000 people signed up, and nearly 1,000 attended. Many of them later requested a Gong product demo, driving serious business for the company.

"Mid-webinar, I realized I was squatting in a meeting room I hadn't booked. I got kicked out and ended up running through the halls, broadcasting from my laptop while 1,000 people waited for me to find another room," Chris chuckles.

Interesting & Timely

Your audience must care about the topic, and the content should arrive when they need it most.

"Our *CFO Letter* piece couldn't have come at a better time," recalled Devin Reed, who took over content marketing at Gong when Chris transitioned to sales. "At the start of the COVID pandemic, I heard salespeople mentioning that CFOs were stepping into every deal. I realized many others were likely facing the same challenge, so we created a timely how-to guide to help them navigate these new gatekeepers."

The *CFO Letter* became one of Gong's most popular assets, with thousands of downloads from salespeople who needed it right then. If your content creates a sense of urgency—encouraging the audience to engage immediately—you'll see much more interaction with it.

Immediately Applicable

With attention spans shrinking—down from 150 seconds in 2004 to just 47 seconds in 2023[20]—your audience needs to see immediate value in your content.

Gone are the days when 40-page e-books or 45-minute lectures captured widespread attention. Instead, snackable content reigns. A 300-word LinkedIn post explaining a data chart, a 45-second video sharing a practical insight, or a 10-item checklist to get a job done are far more likely to be consumed.

---

[20] "Why Our Attention Spans Are Shrinking, with Gloria Mark, PhD," American Psychological Association, February 2023, https://www.apa.org/news/podcasts/speaking-of-psychology/attention-spans.

TikTok creators are excelling with 15-second videos, while younger audiences often prefer a 5-minute YouTube tutorial over a 200-page book. (You are the exception to the rule!)

Follow these principles, and you're likely to create great content. But that's only half the battle. The second half is about ensuring your target audience consumes your content through effective packaging and distribution.

Content Packaging and Distribution

Have you ever spent weeks or even months developing, writing, designing, and perfecting a content piece, only to realize you didn't leave enough time to seriously think about how you're going to get eyeballs on it? If you have, you're not alone.

Content marketers often underestimate the effort needed to create effective landing pages, emails, social media posts, promo videos, and digital ads for their content pieces. I suspect this happens because most of the team's brainpower is allocated to creating a great asset, thinking that packaging and distribution are pretty routine, which in some cases they are. But to create an effective campaign, they can't be an afterthought.

The surprising truth is most of the important content success metrics like content downloads, email opens, and ad clickthroughs *have nothing to do* with the content itself—they are exclusively determined by the packaging. Your email subject line dictates your open rates. The ad headline is responsible for clickthroughs. Your landing page's text and layout determine how many leads convert on it.

In reality, a great content campaign consists of two equally important parts: the content and the packaging. So plan accordingly and allocate 50% of the time and brainpower to each part of the campaign.

How do you nail content packaging? Here are some tips that truly make a difference.

Highlight your great content. First, make sure the three attributes of your content—relevant, interesting, and immediately applicable—shine through in your email subject lines, ad headlines, and landing pages. Address your audience explicitly, create a sense of urgency for consuming the content, and promise your readers a quick win. Effective examples look like this:

- *Get through your buyer's CFO with this template*
- *The sales negotiation mistake you're probably making*
- *No effing way—how cursing impacts sales*

All campaign elements must agree with each other. Have you ever clicked a banner ad promising a content download, only to be served a landing page offering a free product trial? This is lazy marketing. Someone was trying to reuse a landing page with different ad creatives and the result was a "Frankenstein" campaign.

When promoting a content piece, make sure to use the same offer, title, imagery, color palette, and fonts on all the digital ads, emails, landing pages, and the content asset itself. This will improve campaign performance because your audience will feel at ease navigating through the campaign elements, never wondering whether they're in the right place or resenting you for a "bait and switch."

Sell the sizzle, not the steak. The goal of the promotion plan is *not* to sell your product, it's to get folks to consume your content. You need to stay laser-focused on the content-consumption goal as you're copywriting your email subject line and other promotional assets. Intrigue and mystery work well here: "The one thing that will forever change how you coach your team," "We couldn't believe what the data said about cursing on sales calls," or "Our lawyers made us do this" (remember the 39.5% email open rate from Chapter 4?).

Use only relevant images. If you're promoting a cheat sheet, include a thumbnail version of it on the landing page or email to help your audience visualize what they're signing up for. Don't waste that expensive real estate on stock photos of people shaking hands—it's corny and pointless. There's almost always a way of helping your buyers visualize what they'll be getting. Even an e-book can be visualized as a hardcover report for the sake of a landing page. Promoting a gated video or webinar? Show a preview screen or snippet with an exciting chart or key moment in the video, which will make their mouths water in anticipation.

Employee activation. This is a great way to get audience reach beyond your budget. Get every employee of your company to share and engage with meaningful content pieces you produce. This will signal to the social media feed algorithms lots of engagement with your content, which in turn, will make your content more visible on the feed, organically reaching more prospects and customers.

As with most areas of marketing, constantly be testing. Should you add "[PDF]" to the email subject line for higher open rates? Should you capitalize each word? Should it be in question format? Honestly, I don't know. We test these things every chance we get, and we're often surprised by the results.

Consumer behavior and social media algorithms change over time, and many factors will be unique to your business, industry, and geography. Don't miss a good opportunity to test your best subject lines or ad creatives.

Marketing lives in a mostly digital world and testing has never been cheaper or easier. In a matter of days or even hours, you can figure out which creative works best and increase your campaign performance.

To illustrate how my team produced great content coupled with effective distribution, let's visit the Gong Labs story.

Case Study: Gong Labs

When I joined Gong it had only 12 prior employees, including the two co-founders. Coincidentally, it had the same number of companies using its product. When 11 of the 12 beta users turned into paying customers, Amit Bendov, the CEO, called me and asked if I'd come on board to lead marketing.

Having worked with Amit twice before at other companies, I replied, "What took you so long?"

As employee number 13 and marketer number 1, I needed to quickly figure out a content strategy to engage sales leaders we wanted to sell our product to. Browsing through Amazon's book catalog, I easily found more than 100,000 books on sales. Did the world really need more content on sales? Turns out it did.

Most sales content up to that point described one person's experience in sales and their lessons based on that experience. Gong had analyzed sales calls from early customers, looking for patterns of what made an effective conversation, resulting in a won deal. These insights were intended to enrich our software product but an unintended consequence was they provided the perfect materials on which to base a highly effective content strategy.

On my first day at work, I asked my CEO what content he had, that I could use to start generating leads for our business. The only thing he produced was a five-slide deck showing early insights from analyzing customer calls. For example, salespeople who spoke less and listened more were more likely to secure a second call with the prospect than those who dominated the conversation.

I took the simple deck, added a catchy title: "5 Pitching Secrets of Top Sales Pros," and saved the deck as a PDF. Gong's first ebook was created.

Here's an actual page from that first ebook:

SECRET #1: SHUT THE F*CK UP

Top closers spend the most time listening and the least time talking.

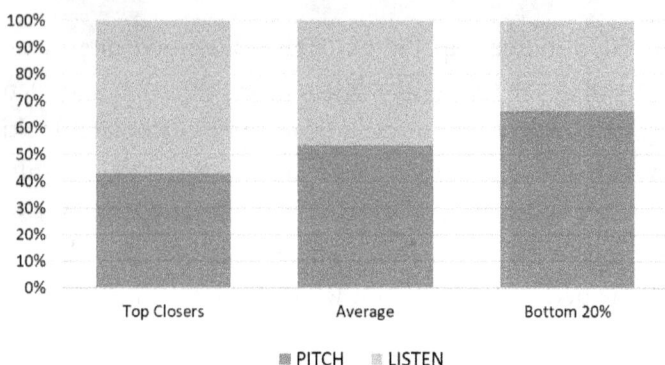

I sent the ebook to a small email list and posted it on social media. Several people downloaded the piece and commented on it. For many, it confirmed long-held beliefs on how salespeople should conduct themselves while, for others, it was a starting point for a good argument. It was a great reminder of the golden rule of content: the worst response is indifference.

Having some people love it and others hate it makes for excellent engagement, something every content team strives for. If it's not offensive to anyone, it probably isn't exciting to anyone, either. Indifference is the only inexcusable response, usually stemming from content watered down for agreeability.

Shortly after launching, we gave our content series a catchy name, "Gong Labs," to allude to its scientific nature. While it was not peer-reviewed like academic publications mandate, it held a high standard of data-backed content, which was relatively new to the B2B marketing world. We found that reporting on arguable sales practices, such as the best way to start a cold call, when to use apologetic language, whether to swear, and how long to shut up after presenting pricing, made very engaging content.

To package our content in a fun way our audience wanted to consume, we struck a healthy balance of credible education and light entertainment, otherwise known as *"edutainment."* This style of content with substance delivered in a tone that isn't deadly serious has become increasingly popular on social media and makes potentially boring content exciting and easy to consume.

As the best content marketing does, Gong Labs slyly promoted Gong's software product, without explicitly sounding like a sales pitch. We used this disclaimer at the beginning of dozens of Gong Lab articles:

> "This article is part of the Gong Labs series, where we publish findings from our data research team. We analyze sales conversations and deals using the Gong Revenue Intelligence Platform's proprietary AI, then share the results to help you win more deals."

By admitting "we drank our own champagne," we piqued interest in our product from folks whose guards were down as they were getting value from our content. Every time we used this disclaimer in a new article, we saw product demo requests coming in even though we didn't directly promote our product.

After years of publishing insights on sales *calls*, we acquired a small company that produced similar insights on sales *emails*. After publishing our first article analyzing the effectiveness of different types of sales emails, we saw an influx of interest in our updated product, which happened to analyze emails, as well.

Gong Labs hit all the attributes of great content: it was hyper-**relevant** to sales professionals, **interesting** and **timely** as it helped them with daily challenges like conducting better sales calls and composing effective sales emails, and we made sure it was always **immediately consumable** by slicing and dicing our content into snackable bites our audience could consume in just a few minutes before putting the newly learned insight or skill to work.

A fun example[21]: "How have you been?" is the most effective cold-call opener compared to popular alternatives like "Did I catch you at a bad time?" or "How are you?" (Note that the "best opener" likely changes over time and geographies, so always be testing.)

Employee activation was another force multiplier in distributing Gong Labs: we regularly orchestrated "LinkedIn takeovers," in which hundreds of Gong employees shared freshly released articles to increase their reach. I am often asked how we orchestrated so many Gong employees sharing our content. When I tell folks we never used any secret technology or tool for this,

---

[21] Chris Orlob, "Effective Cold Call Opening Lines: Data-Driven Insights," Gong Labs, April 19, 2018, https://www.gong.io/resources/labs/cold-call-opening-lines/.

their minds are blown. The actual method we used couldn't be simpler: Like any effective call to action, we made it easy to do and clarified to our team "what's in it for me" (WIIFM).

We sent all employees a calendar block, an email, and a Slack message for the exact moment we wanted them to share the content. We included a simple-to-follow template they could use verbatim if they didn't have the time or will to write their own take on the content but could also be personalized by those with a stronger point of view.

To clarify the WIIFM, I frequently explained to our employees how the LinkedIn feed algorithm favors content pieces that get a lot of engagement shortly after they're published. This increased engagement made our content more visible to prospects and customers, which we then transformed into qualified buyer meetings—every salesperson's dream.

Our strategy for converting anonymous readers from social media to sales opportunities was so straightforward I'm surprised more brands didn't adopt it sooner. When we published Gong Labs articles, we optimized for audience reach, keeping them ungated and promoted in the public domain—mostly on organic social media channels, in our email program, and through employee activation.

Once readers reached halfway through the article, they would find a link to a related, premium content piece. When they clicked through, they arrived on a simple landing page, which collected their contact details before granting access to the premium content. So an article on buyers' freezing budgets led to a premium asset on how to get past your buyer's CFO. Similarly, a content piece on effective email calls-to-action linked to a list of 43 irresistible email CTAs.

By cleverly creating premium content, which was a natural extension of the public-domain article on LinkedIn, we caught our audience members while they were "in the zone" of learning more about a topic, resulting in very high conversion rates on our landing pages—70 to 80% in some cases.

The secret to making this work was ensuring the ungated article provided enough independent value, without requiring readers to submit their email addresses. When we crossed that line and tried posting just the beginning of the article on social media and required folks to enter their email to read the meaty part of the article, we experienced a backlash of low conversion rates on our landing page. Unsurprisingly in hindsight, folks didn't appreciate the bait and switch.

Once we captured contacts' emails on our landing pages, we included them in email drip campaigns, alerting our sales team when a lead "raised their hand," indicating they were ready for a sales call.

Lastly, we focused all our efforts on a single platform. I'm not suggesting this is the best choice for *every* business. But after some initial testing of other platforms like X (formerly Twitter) and Facebook, we quickly discovered our target audience of salespeople was mostly active on LinkedIn; they were there looking for their next job, candidate, customer, or partner. That's when we decided to concentrate our efforts on a singular platform. We studied the feed algorithm to understand what content types and posting habits it favored and optimized our content for the platform.

A funny example was when I discovered on LinkedIn's engineering blog they were testing a new "dwell factor." Essentially, they were rewarding posts that kept users' attention for a long time and stopped them from scrolling down their feeds.

I had the childish idea of asking my team to create a "Where's Waldo?" sort of image hiding our mascot, Bruno the bulldog, instead of Waldo. That post performed exceptionally well as folks stopped scrolling and looked for our bulldog for several long minutes.

Gong has been fortunate to hire some of the industry's best sales and marketing stars. Once we identified some of these team members were comfortable creating content on social media, we leaned into those efforts and gave them marketing support.

Sarah Brazier, a sales development representative (SDR) got her own mini-series we produced, following her journey from SDR to account executive. And Caspian Lewke became known as "the king of memes" for his witty sales-related memes, which marketing amplified to the delight of our followers.

These efforts not only helped us reach a broader audience than marketing could have without the help of additional content creators, it also portrayed Gong as a fun place to work with awesome team members.

Raising the Bar for Content Quality

Let's assume you put in the work to create what you think might be great content. Maybe you even invested in a thorough distribution plan. But how can you be sure your content is great?

At Gong, we set two bars for content quality. The first was to ask, would you consume your own content? Before hitting that "send" or "post" button, every marketer needs to ask themselves, "Would I consume this content if I didn't work here?" If the answer is anything short of a "heck, yeah!" you'll probably want to review that content again to see if you can make it more exciting or table it until you have something better.

You only get so many chances to engage your audience and if you burn through them with mediocre content one too many times, they will unsubscribe and unfollow you, stripping your right to communicate with them.

The second, higher bar, is whether people would pay for your content. If that sounds unrealistic at first, ask yourself: do you pay for content from Netflix, Spotify, MasterClass, or *The New York Times*? If you do, you're already paying for quality content. Is your marketing content worthy of someone's hard-earned dollars?

While we never directly monetized our content (we were in the software business and our content was a means to an end), we always celebrated moments when it was clear we'd hit that high bar of content so good people would pay for it. Two examples include a sales professor at a U.S. university, asking how much we would charge her to use our content in her sales course. A similar request came from a Head of Sales Enablement who inquired about repurposing our content for her training needs.

We declined payment from all these requests and asked only that they attribute the content to Gong. These are real-life examples of B2B marketing content so good people have been willing to pay for it.

Content marketing is the single most effective organic growth tactic for most B2B startups. To fully exploit it, ensure it contains the three elements of great content and follow the guidelines for a solid packaging and distribution plan. Finally, inspire your team to create content they would consume and others would pay for.

Taking a sharp turn from the most cost-effective to the most expensive—but effective—marketing tactic, our next chapter will explore event marketing, from sponsoring a small booth at a conference to creating your own show. There are many ways of making these big investments worth your while, resulting in sales pipeline and revenue.

CHAPTER 7

CREATING EVENTS MAGIC

"Part of show business is magic.
You don't know how it happens."

—Sammy Davis, Jr.

"4,567 leads." Ariel, my marketing automation guy, looked up from his laptop.

"Are you sure?" I asked. 4,567 sounded too perfect a number, and a new record, to be the number of leads we collected at our booth at Oracle OpenWorld, a trade show we recently attended.

"I imported the list from the lead scanners and de-duplicated them myself!" Ariel responded with pride.

Months before exhibiting at Oracle OpenWorld, our team sat down to discuss the results of a previous trade show, where we collected 300 sales leads. Not bad for a small booth at a medium-sized show. "What would it take to come back with 1,000 leads?" asked Amit, my CMO. I was the VP of Marketing at Panaya at the time, where planning and running our trade shows was my responsibility.

We carefully analyzed what drew attendees to a specific booth—from the booth's location, size, height, and graphic design, through the activities held in the booth and staff interactions, to the giveaway we handed out—and formulated a new strategy.

We blew our 1,000-lead target out of the water, returning with 4,567 leads, which converted into dozens of new customers, ringing in a handsome, seven-figure revenue number and a 10x return on our investment in the show. We accomplished this at a short, three-day show with eight staffers and thousands of teddy bears. But I'm getting ahead of myself.

Events are the most interactive and personable touch points a marketing team can create. Even in this digital world we're living in and after virtual events took off during the COVID pandemic (only to quickly subside), customers and prospects haven't given up on the intimate and human-centric experience of a great event.

As any salesperson who's ever met a prospect at a trade show and shared drinks with them at the hotel bar will tell you, these in-person meetings lubricate sales and build rapport better than any other type of encounter.

Most of this chapter is a better-written, briefer version of a short book I published in 2015, *The 50 Secrets of Trade Show Success*. As such, it contains a mixture of both the basics of planning and running a great show and inspiring, creative examples of pulling off press-worthy stunts at big industry events. If events aren't really your thing, feel free to come back to it as a reference when you need it and move on to the next chapter, in which I share some horror stories of things gone terribly wrong.

Pick (or Hijack) the Right Show

The best rule for choosing the right shows is to focus on those narrowly targeting your audience and pick the largest ones.

Go to shows with an audience too broad and you're wasting your time on 70 or 80 percent of booth visitors who aren't potential buyers. Go to well-targeted but small shows and you'll end up meeting only a handful of buyers.

To determine the overlap of your target audience and show attendees, ask the organizer for detailed firmographics and demographics of previous shows' attendees. Look at the breakdown by:

- Business function (e.g., Marketing, HR, or Sales)
- Seniority (e.g., Director, VP, or CXO)
- Company size
- Industry
- Geography

Don't settle for this year's expected turnout. Ask for the previous show's actual numbers. If you're sponsoring an inaugural show with no past attendance benchmarks, you should expect to pay a low sponsorship price for the trust you're placing in the organizer.

All other things being equal, opt for a show where you can secure a speaking opportunity. Getting 20 to 45 minutes in front of a captive audience can go a long way toward strengthening your brand and driving people to your booth.

I've gone as far as sponsoring a show where I got a speaking opportunity and declined the booth because I couldn't design and staff it in time. Attendees posted key moments of my presentation on social media, which was far more valuable than a few folks walking home with our booth giveaways. Pro tip: create content so good that the event organizers invite you to speak on their dime, without having to sponsor the show.

As an early-stage startup, you'll often find great shows outside your budget's sponsorship reach. An alternative to consider is creatively "hijacking" foot traffic at these shows. Freshworks, a Salesforce competitor, hijacked attention from the incumbent's largest trade show, Dreamforce. It branded a giant blimp with #failforce and flew it above Salesforce Tower, the iconic company's headquarters[22]. The blimp was visible to thousands of Dreamforce attendees who amplified their amusement with it on social media and in the press.

You could call the #failsforce blimp poetic justice as Salesforce founder Marc Benioff was no stranger to picking on larger competitors on their home court. In the early Salesforce days, Benioff staged a "protest" (in reality, paid actors) outside the Siebel User Conference[23] in San Francisco. The protestors were calling to end on-premise software in favor of software-as-a-service (SaaS). The stunt got huge media attention, propelling the Salesforce brand.

---

[22] "#Failsforce Blimp by Freshworks," YouTube, September 26, 2018, https://www.youtube.com/watch?v=_fmXl-Aj5LQ.

[23] Zachary Minott, "The Staged Protest That Kickstarted the Growth of Salesforce Into a Billion-Dollar Company," Medium, October 22, 2020, https://ehandbook.com/the-staged-protest-that-kickstarted-the-growth-of-salesforce-into-a-billion-dollar-company-a53d6995f762.

Standing on the shoulders of giants, we staged a few trade show stunts during my time at Gong. The first was at another Dreamforce show. As I shared when discussing our category-creation efforts, we couldn't afford to sponsor the show, so we paid a modest amount to wrap 20 ride-share cars with our new category message, "Goodbye Opinions, Hello Reality." The drivers were paid extra to pick up and drop off Dreamforce attendees. Hundreds of passengers rode in these "Gong cars" and many posted their photos on social media, amplifying our small investment to a sizable audience.

During the same event, we took over the nearby Montgomery transportation station, branding it with Gong visuals—on the station's floor, screens, and floor-to-ceiling columns. Thousands of Dreamforce attendees were immersed in our branding even before setting foot in the show.

After choosing or highjacking the right show, it's time to define your goal.

Pick a Goal, Any Goal

You should focus on one big goal per show. If absolutely necessary, pick a secondary goal, but no more. Try to juggle too many balls and you're sure to drop a few. Your goal and Key Performance Indicators (KPIs) will inform your booth design, so it's important to get them right.

Common goals for booth design are: lead generation, meeting decision makers, meeting customers and prospects, and brand awareness. Let's unpack each of these.

Lead generation. Keeping the 95-5 rule in mind, design the booth to attract target buyers, whether or not they're currently in the market. The easiest way to do this is with a broad-appeal attraction like a game or raffle. Think of simple games like dart-throwing, slot machines, or a wheel of fortune to maximize traffic at your booth. Once you scan the leads, you can nurture them with helpful content, keeping you top-of-mind, until they're ready to buy.

Another way of maximizing booth traffic for lead generation is handing out food or beverages. Having the best coffee machine, an open bar in the later hours of the day, or an irresistible popcorn cart will have visitors lining up.

Common KPIs for this type of booth are:

- Number of leads scanned.
- Number of leads scanned by each staff member per day—make it a friendly competition!
- Number of *new* accounts and contacts scanned.

One year at a large IT show, SAP Sapphire, we stood out by designing our booth as a cruise ship. We had live palm trees, a huge cruise ship backdrop, and a bartender crafting mocktails. Visitors lined up from land to sea (I'll put a dollar in the jar for that one).

Meeting decision makers. At some point, you'll find yourself exhibiting at the same trade show annually and scanning visitors from the same companies over and over again. One way of getting more out of this situation is to use a game for identifying decision-makers in real time, so your staff can approach them, skipping less qualified visitors.

To identify decision-makers, my team developed self-qualifying computer games, but you can rent game stations and use phone apps to alert your booth staff when a qualified buyer is present. The idea behind these games is simple: visitors are drawn in for a chance to win a prize. To play the game, they are asked to enter a few personal details on a tablet or laptop. These details are cross-referenced against your target buyer list and alert booth staff to have a conversation with decision makers.

A good KPI for this booth setup is the number of conversations held with decision-makers.

Meeting customers and prospects. To do this well, you'll want to set up an in-booth meeting area. If you install see-through walls around the meeting area, your booth will look busy during meetings and passersby will want in on the action. Off-booth meeting rooms are often too far away from the show floor and difficult to drag visitors to, so setting up a dedicated meeting area at your booth is your best bet for ensuring these meetings happen.

An effective way of ensuring your salespeople pre-schedule meetings is to set a target number of meetings they must schedule before earning the right to travel to the show.

A good KPI for this booth setup is the number of meetings held.

Brand awareness. This is best achieved *outside* your booth, by securing a keynote, breakout, or panel speaking opportunity. These sessions build brand authority and drive people to your booth. Use booth graphics to boost brand awareness and set up press and analyst meetings to share your latest product news.

Good KPIs for this type of booth are the number of attendees at your speaking session and the number of media contacts and industry analysts briefed.

Now that your goals are set, let's turn our attention to the different types of booth configurations and when you might want to pick each one.

Booth Configurations

Your booth type makes a huge difference to your visibility, the price you pay, and the traffic you'll draw. Let's examine the four common booth types: aisle, corner, peninsula, and island.

CORNER	AISLE	AISLE	AISLE	CORNER
CORNER	AISLE	AISLE	AISLE	CORNER

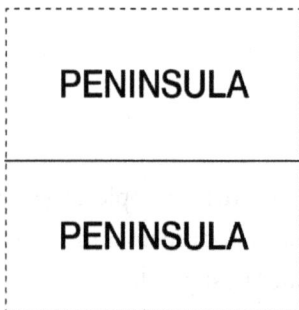

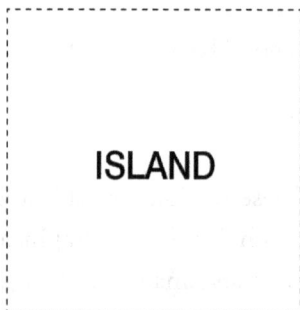

PENINSULA
PENINSULA

ISLAND

Aisle

With three walls and an open side, the aisle is also known as an inline booth. This is the most cost-effective configuration with plenty of wall space for messaging and shelving but it has limited visibility.

Corner

The corner booth is located on an aisle corner with two walls and two open sides. It costs more due to its scarcity and increased visibility.

Peninsula

As its name suggests, this type includes one wall and three open sides. This configuration has great visibility and foot traffic from three aisles, but it's more expensive than an aisle or corner booth.

Island

Located at a crossroad with no walls and four open sides, the island has the ultimate visibility and can often be built taller than other booths, further increasing its visibility. You can build anything you can dream of in this space, which makes it the most expensive configuration. It usually requires professional labor for set-up and break-down, which also adds cost.

Bottom line: the fewer walls your booth has, the more you'll pay for the space and design but the better your chances of standing out. Bold, creative design can make even the tiniest aisle booth stand out so unless you have the means for it, don't worry about getting the biggest booth at the show.

The next thing is to decide on the giveaways your staff will be handing out to attendees.

Giveaways

We've all been there—it's a month before the show and you're scrambling to find a great giveaway. Common thinking suggests keeping it cheap and slapping a big logo on it. But choosing memorable and effective giveaways will help you close more business. Let's look at some proven giveaway ideas.

Many small prizes work better than one big prize. With prizes, there are two psychological effects at play. First, people crave instant gratification. Studies have shown most people will take $80 now rather than wait a month to receive $100. The same principle is at work here. Most visitors would rather take what they can get now than wait for a larger prize at the end of the day.

Second, most people are risk-averse. Raffling a large prize raises doubts about the raffle's integrity, the odds of winning, and the raffle's timing. That's why I will always opt for small prizes for many visitors if budget and logistics allow.

Cool and useful beats boring. Most booths still hand out mints, pens, and coffee mugs. These usually get tossed in the trash can, if they're picked up at all.

Pick something cool that brings a smile to your visitors' faces. Children's toys, like a remote-controlled drone or a stuffed animal, will save your visitors from buying gifts on their way home. Or go for something useful like a flashlight, an umbrella during rainy weather, or a computer accessory.

Brand tastefully. Printing your company logo on the giveaway adds a nice touch when done appropriately. I've often opted for neon-colored stickers that read "WIN ME AT BOOTH 243" to draw more booth traffic as folks walk around with the branded giveaways.

Show them off. Booth staffers often hide giveaways under counters, sneaking them out only for select visitors. If you chose attractive giveaways visitors love, why hide them?

"Because if I left them out, they'd get stolen!"

If that's the case, consider using photos of your giveaways in your booth's signage, hanging sample giveaways high above the booth, or displaying them on a high, inaccessible shelf. Keep the rest under a counter or in see-through containers for increased visibility. Your prizes aren't going to give themselves away.

Your booth also needs welcoming faces to greet your guests. Let's turn our attention to the best choices for staffing your booth.

Staffing for Success

Most often, sales development representatives (SDRs) and salespeople are the best booth staffers because they're building their own pipeline by collecting new leads. They're also meeting active opportunities and customers that they can upsell. Customer success managers (CSMs) are also good staffers if you expect existing customers to show up.

The best time for training your booth staff is a few days before leaving for the show with a short refresher training before the show opens each morning.

Encourage staff to be outgoing and courteous. They should stand at the outer perimeter of your booth or in the aisle to grab the attention of passersby. Staffers should ask a short question visitors can easily answer "yes" to. If you're looking for IBM clients, you could ask, "Do you use IBM applications?"

Once you determine they're a qualified decision maker, continue the sales process by presenting a product demo and conducting discovery on their needs. If they're unqualified, disengage quickly to free yourself for other visitors.

To appear welcoming, avoid standing behind a table, sitting, eating, drinking, and checking emails at the booth. Exhibitors huddling among themselves also make visitors feel unwelcome.

Hiring temporary local staff is a smart move for saving on travel costs and when you don't have enough employees who speak the local language. Use locals for tasks requiring little knowledge of your product: scanning badges, handing out giveaways and product literature, and ushering people into meeting rooms or demo stations.

With the right booth, at the right show, armed with cool giveaways and a welcoming staff, you're set up for success at the show. To make the most out of your big investment, a thoughtful pre-show campaign can help drive traffic to your booth while a timely post-show campaign will convert your booth attendees to interested buyers.

Pre- & Post-Show Campaigns

You can rely on the show organizer to bring traffic to the show but getting folks to your booth is on you.

Most pre-show emails read something like "Visit our booth at the show! We look forward to seeing you there." Why would I visit their booth? To ensure visitors show up, send email invitations and make calls 7-10 days before the show when most attendees are finalizing their plans. Include a compelling offer, like these:

Personal gift. "Hey Bob, I'll be at the Vegas show next week and have a personal gift for you. Could you stop by Monday morning at 11 AM?"

VIP meeting. "Hey Rachel, my CEO will be at the show next week and has only three meeting slots left. I wanted you to be the first to hear about this opportunity." If one of your employees, customers, or partners is an industry celebrity, use them to draw in a crowd.

Private product demo. This works well with customers who are innovators or early adopters.

Cocktail event. Invite people to a social gathering right after show hours or to an early breakfast event before the show opens.

In your invitation, be precise about the day and time you want to meet: "See you there on Monday at 11 AM?" is more effective than "I hope to see you there."

After the show, the booth team wants to go out and celebrate their hard work. The last thing on anyone's mind is adding notes to scanned leads, updating the CRM, or figuring out which email to send to prospects. But delaying these actions is the difference between effective follow-up and allowing hot leads to go cold.

A successful post-show campaign starts with setting it up *before* the show. This is the best way to ensure it goes out on time. Next, upload the leads to your CRM immediately after the show. (There are purpose-built apps that can do that in real-time while your staff scans the leads[24].) Finally, send the follow-up email in the morning hours of the first business day after the show, before other exhibitors get their act together and do the same.

The follow-up email should jog visitors' memory of the giveaway they received ("I hope your child enjoyed the teddy bear!") and give them another gift, like a valuable piece of content. On the landing page gating the content, ask a few qualifying questions to help your sales team prioritize calls. Send a follow-up email several days later to those who didn't click through the first email.

Take your leads to the next buying step by inviting them to a product demo or a free trial and include them in a nurturing campaign, to keep your brand top-of-mind until they're ready to buy.

So far we've dealt with advice for running an effective booth at an in-person tradeshow. Another event type to consider is virtual events.

Virtual Events

The COVID pandemic gave rise to virtual events in 2020. They have since subsided in popularity but are nevertheless here to stay. Events teams around the world scrambled in the early

---

[24] "The World's First Event-Agnostic Lead Scanner," Mobly, accessed January 25, 2025, https://www.getmobly.com/.

pandemic days to reimagine events as virtual to make up for some of the lost human connection of in-person events.

I'm lucky to have been part of a team that accomplished impossible feats on the regular, so when we learned our planned in-person events couldn't happen, we took a deep breath and figured out how to run a successful virtual event, from A to Z, in two weeks.

Our first event was a tremendous success. While most companies were struggling to figure out if they should go virtual or wait for field events to return, we got 3,000 registrants for our virtual event and 1,200 attendees.

In the following three months, we attended every virtual event in our industry, soaking up every learning we could. By July 2020, we were ready for our second, bigger and better virtual event. This time, we had nearly 4,500 registrants and almost 2,000 attendees with overwhelmingly positive feedback.

Next, we'll dive into some of the top tips and takeaways from our virtual event successes.

Content, Experience, & Promotion

The crucial pillars of a virtual event's success are stellar content, attendee experience, and your strategy for promoting the event.

A great virtual event has a tight theme designed for a uniform audience. Don't try catering to the interests of multiple audiences or few will show up. The entire day's agenda should read as if it was created for a single, specific attendee persona. If your business sells to multiple personas, host a separate event or track for each.

A mix of celebrity speakers like authors and athletes combined with leading industry practitioners and our own company's research and product updates yielded the best audience engagement. Keep content sessions short—ideally, 20-30 minutes. Allow 45 minutes for a larger panel but run any longer and you risk losing your audience.

As on social media, your audience is looking for an inspiring mix of education and entertainment. Aside from the world-class content, we also included a live DJ during the reception, breaks, and happy hour. We had a live magic act with audience participation and closed out the day with an interactive mixology class for our executive happy hour. All these created delightful moments our audience gushed over.

Another audience favorite was live networking opportunities between attendees. This was a digital reimagination of those random show floor moments folks missed from in-person events. Most virtual event platforms cater for this functionality, so consider using it.

A behind-the-scenes tip to keep in mind is virtual events have a lot of technical moving parts. With unpredictable internet speeds and broadcasting from multiple locations, some things are bound to break. We created a "we'll be right back!" slide for technical difficulty moments and made good use of it in our first virtual event.

Have dedicated people running the show so the speakers are not multitasking. Attendees expect you to stick to the schedule, so time and rehearse all sessions. Consider pre-recording non-interactive sessions to reduce the risk of technical issues, but incorporate enough interactive sessions to keep things alive and engaging.

Our best promotion channels, as measured by tickets claimed, were organic social media promotion, especially on LinkedIn, and email invites to our "house list." Each post and email focused on a different benefit of the event—a star speaker, live entertainment, raffle prizes, etc. We even sold five event sponsorships to non-competing companies who promoted the event to their audience and covered most of our costs.

Measuring Event Success

Given events are some of the biggest marketing investments, your CEO and CFO will expect you to measure and demonstrate their impact on the business. There are different approaches to measuring return on investment (ROI) including marketing attribution models and marketing media mix (MMM). I won't attempt to cover them all but I'll provide a few metrics and approaches I've found useful.

Leading KPIs:

- Number of accounts influenced
- Number of new accounts met
- Number of contacts influenced
- Number of new contacts met
- Number of active opportunities influenced
- Number of new opportunities sourced
- Number of customer meetings held
- Number of attendees at speaking sessions

Lagging KPIs to track a few months after the show:

- Number of new deals won
- Dollar amount of deals won
- Average deal size
- Deal velocity

With the right KPIs tracked, you're ready to move on to calculate event ROI. I've seen success with three methods; each has its pros and cons.

Active Opportunities: This approach looks at cohorts of active opportunities during, say, a given quarter. Some opportunities had a contact attend an event and others did not. Compare the behavior and outcome of those who attended with those who did not:

- How fast are deals closing when a contact attends an event vs. when they don't?
- How much faster do deals progress?
- Does average deal size grow as a result of event attendance?

Finding a clear impact on even one of these metrics makes a compelling case for your events budget. During one event season at Gong, we found contacts from active opportunities attending our events doubled the average deal size and win rates, demonstrating clear ROI.

Conservative ROI: This approach is straightforward to present to management. All you need are two metrics:

- Dollars from Won Opportunities
- Dollars Invested

The equation is simple:

$$[Conservative\ ROI] =$$
$$[Dollars\ from\ Won\ Opportunities] - [Dollars\ Invested]$$

If you invested $200,000 in your booth and the business attributed to the show amounted to $500,000, your show's Conservative ROI is:

$$\$500,000 - \$200,000 = \$300,000$$

While calculating Conservative ROI is quick and easy to communicate, the reality is often more complex, creating the need for a less conservative ROI calculation.

Liberal ROI: If you track opportunities created from a show over time, you'll notice many opportunities have not yet matured into a deal. Liberal ROI attempts to place a value on open opportunities and new accounts and leads met at the show.

To calculate this more realistic, liberal ROI, you need a good history of past opportunities, average deal sizes, and conversion rates between them.

Say your company's average deal size is $50,000 and 1 out of 5 qualified leads results in a won deal. That's a 20% conversion rate. This allows us to place a value on a qualified lead: it is $10,000 because 5 qualified leads equal 1 deal won. Since the average deal size is $50,000, this is also the value of 5 qualified leads, which means a single qualified lead is worth $10,000.

Using the same approach, estimate the value of a show lead. If your company qualified 1 in 10 event leads and a qualified lead is valued $10,000, we now know 10 event leads are worth $10,000.

In other words, each event lead is worth $1,000. That's all there is to it. Using this method with your company's historical data, you can calculate the value of leads, accounts, qualified leads, and opportunities.

Once you have these estimated values, you're ready to calculate your trade show's Liberal ROI. Here's the equation:

$$
\begin{bmatrix} \text{Liberal ROI} \end{bmatrix} = \begin{bmatrix} \text{Dollars from Won} \\ \text{Opportunities} \end{bmatrix} + \begin{bmatrix} \textbf{Estimated Value of:} \\ \text{All Leads} \\ \text{New Leads} \\ \text{All Accounts} \\ \text{New Accounts} \\ \text{Customer Meetings} \\ \text{Qualified Leads} \\ \text{Opportunities} \end{bmatrix} - \begin{bmatrix} \text{Dollars Invested} \end{bmatrix}
$$

This looks scary, so don't try using all suggested metrics at once. It's better to choose one or two metrics you have good data for and use only those to calculate liberal ROI. The value of active opportunities, not yet won, is a good starting point.

Events have always been a meaningful opportunity to meet prospects, customers, and partners in person and, more recently, virtually, to create connections and explore mutual opportunities. Unfortunately, these events come at a high cost. Planning and executing them with careful attention and care will ensure you'll maximize your return on these investments.

Start by picking the right shows and then decide between sponsoring and highjacking their foot traffic with a creative PR stunt. Set your goal for the show and optimize your booth configuration and layout to achieve it (e.g., game stations for lead generation). Hand out cool or useful giveaways—anything but boring. Staff your booth with salespeople and SDRs who've been prepped for success. Ensure your pre-show campaign gives visitors a solid reason to meet you at the booth and prepare the post-show campaign to go out as soon as the show ends.

Virtual events' success leans on content and attendee experience. Promote those, and you will create a truly delightful time for your guests. Plan ahead for the inevitable technical glitches, and don't sweat it in real time. Your audience will understand and support you.

Choose one of three methods of measuring event ROI and calculate a few basic metrics to get a starting point you can share with your CFO and head of sales, demonstrating how events are contributing to the business. Evolve your ROI calculations over time as you develop the measurement muscle.

The last few chapters covered marketing tactics for impactful brand campaigns, category creation, content marketing, and events. Reading through inspiring stories of other CMOs and my own team, you might be impressed with how we seemingly went from one success to the next.

But not everything went as planned. Since learning from my mistakes and those of others has been so crucial to my personal growth, our next chapter will cover two monumental mistakes I made and what I learned from them.

CHAPTER 8

WHEN THINGS GO WRONG

*"Mistakes are the proof that we are human and flawed,
but also capable of growth and improvement."*

—Brené Brown

"Shockingly tone-deaf and self-serving," "gross," and "one of the most offensive things I've seen," were just three of the customer responses my CEO and board members forwarded to me moments after my email campaign went out.

In June 2020, many Americans were discussing the horrific murder of George Floyd, which led to the rise of the Black Lives Matter movement. My marketing team wanted to support the movement by donating money to an organization promoting BLM causes and, if possible, get some good publicity points on the way.

We came up with an email campaign we sent to 6,000 customers suggesting that Gong would donate $10 to the National Association for the Advancement of Colored People (NAACP) for every review our customers wrote about Gong on G2, a popular software reviews site. Past campaigns, where we offered customers a gift card in exchange for a review, were very well-received.

We sincerely wanted to donate money to a good cause and invited our customers to join us on the journey. What could possibly go wrong?

Quite a lot, as it turned out.

This was the email we sent out to 6,000 Gong users:

Subject: We'll make a donation in your name

Jason,

This past week has forced some reflection on all of us.

And it got us thinking: how can we help make an impact on ending systemic racism?

Here's what we came up with, and I hope you like it.

We'd like to make a donation in your name to the **NAACP.**

To make this happen, all we ask is that you <u>leave a short review of Gong here.</u>

We've partnered with G2, so that with every review that comes in, G2 and Gong will *each* be making **$10 donations** to the organization on your behalf.

At Gong, we set a lofty goal of hitting $5,000 in donations by the end of the week.

Thanks for playing your part, and keep fighting the good fight.

PS: if you have other suggestions for how we can help, just hit *Reply*.

Within an hour, we received six livid responses. Our customers called us tone-deaf and were disappointed with us tying our donation to the NAACP to them writing a review for us. One or two threatened to cut ties altogether. My CEO got one email directly from a customer. A board member forwarded another angry response to my CEO.

I had clearly messed up by approving this campaign in the first place. I quickly contemplated my options: I could do nothing, hoping the handful of angry responses would subside and everyone would go on with their day; or I could own up to my mistake, risking giving it even more publicity, but ultimately letting our customers know that we realized our mistake and were doing something to correct it.

Knowing what I do about consumer behavior, I had an unshakeable hunch that behind every one of the six customers who found the time and words to write us an angry, disappointed response, there were probably 10 to 20 others who felt the same anger but didn't find the time or words to let us know about it.

I made the call and within a couple hours of receiving that first email response, we sent out an apology email to all 6,000 customers who'd received the original email, only this time it came from my personal email address.

From: Udi Ledergor

Subject: I messed up

Jason,

I made a bad call.

Earlier today, you received an email from us asking you to review Gong on G2 knowing that it would result in a donation in your name to the NAACP.

That was poor judgment on my part.

I wanted to update you and let you know we decided to make this right.

We are making an immediate unconditional donation of $25,000 to be divided between these 4 organizations whose important work we want to support:

- Black Lives Matter
- Trans Gender District
- Boris Henson Foundation
- NAACP

I also want to thank you for your valuable feedback and understanding that our intentions were genuinely different from how they came out.

I'm happy to continue the conversation with you at any time. Just drop me a line.

Thanks for pushing us to make things right and holding us accountable.

Udi
Chief Marketing Officer

Within moments, my email inbox was flooded. I received 66 responses to the apology email. That's 11 times the number of complaint emails the original campaign received. Every one of the 66 emails was positive.

Some customers wrote in to say they didn't find anything wrong with the original email. But most of them wrote to thank me for owning up to my mistake and making things right. They admitted that something about the original email felt wrong and that they couldn't quite express it in words. They were all very appreciative of receiving the apology email.

As I reflect on the events of that day, three important learnings come to mind:

1. Give-and-take plays are common in sales and marketing and usually, everyone will cooperate with them. However, when sensitive social issues are at stake, such a play can ratchet up raw emotions. Even alluding to anything with the optics of a transaction required for someone to do the right thing can severely backfire.

   We could have just donated to the social organizations we wanted to support, with or without making it public. Everyone would have supported us in doing so. It was tying our donation to the request that customers review us on G2 that sent tone-deaf signals, triggering the upset responses.

2. Even a handful of negative responses can indicate a much larger group of upset customers that, for some reason or another, didn't find the time or energy to let us know how they feel. I had a strong hunch that the six

negative responses I received were indicative of a much larger group. The subsequent 66 positive responses to my apology proved I was right.

3. Speed matters. The fact that we acted quickly and sent out an apology within a couple of hours of realizing what we did wrong made a huge difference. Deliberating on it for days or hoping that the problem would go away could have done a lot more damage.

   Customers would have marinated on their negative feelings toward us and could have aired them on social media, sending even more angry responses to my CEO and board members, or actually cutting their business ties with Gong. My swift action put out the fire quickly and gave customers instant relief that they had been heard and that corrective action was taken. Phew.

No Second Touchdown

On the heels of our 2021 Super Bowl commercial's success, when we set a new record for weekly sales pipeline creation, I was eager to recreate and surpass that success with a bigger, better 2022 Super Bowl campaign. I managed to secure a budget three times bigger than the first big-game experiment and set out to create a memorable commercial.

I repeated a similar regional media buy, so the main difference between our two Super Bowl campaigns was the ad creative. With a larger budget in hand, I hired a professional agency that had worked with big brand names and had produced high-profile commercials, including several for the Super Bowl.

The agency worked on our brief and presented us with four creative directions. We really liked one of them, which involved hiring a big celebrity who was a household name. That would have definitely gotten people talking about our commercial but the budget we'd need to get him seemed out of our reach. We settled on our second-favorite creative concept, which involved a huge set, dozens of actors, gymnasts, extras, and props—including many gongs of all sizes.

To watch the commercial, go to this link or scan the QR code below:

bit.ly/udisflop

It was a Super Bowl-worthy extravaganza. It was also mostly a waste of money and energy. We failed to recreate the publicity and business success of our first big-game commercial. Social media buzz around our commercial was much weaker than the previous year's, and we came up short on the game-day website traffic spike and subsequent sales pipeline.

A combination of several factors contributed to this flop. Here are the main ones I identified:

1. We enjoyed the element of surprise in the first year, which wasn't such a surprise the second time around. I underestimated the impact of this element, which was now seen as just another channel we were advertising on.

2. I ignored the best piece of advice I got from a fellow CMO which I had implemented in the first commercial: show the damn product. Talk about how it helps. Showcasing the product and its impact in our first commercial drove people to our website and increased positive awareness of our brand. Our second commercial was a three-ring circus of visual and audible gags but explained nothing about the product. Larger brands—like insurance companies and beverage manufacturers—can afford to do this, because they are household names. Nobody needs Budweiser to explain how their product is used. Gong was nowhere near that level of brand recognition, which led to our ad falling flat.

3. Getting a big-name celebrity might have made a world of difference and helped us cut through the noise. I don't know for certain that we could have secured the necessary budget, but I should have explored that route more seriously.

Needless to say, that was the last Super Bowl commercial I had the courage to ask to budget for.

There are countless ways to get things wrong, so learning from your mistakes and those of others can be valuable. I like to treat failures as learning moments: I just figured out something doesn't work. That narrows down the list of things I'll try next, which might work.

Not enough attendees showed up at our event? Let's analyze the promo campaigns, content, and speaker lineup, and target attendees to learn what we could have done better.

A new content piece fell flat with our audience? Let's reverse-engineer the timing, topic, execution, and distribution to identify weaknesses we can improve on for our next release.

As anyone who's ever accomplished anything will honestly admit, I've failed an order of magnitude more times than I've succeeded. Luckily, some of those successes were great enough to cover for the failures and none of the failures were career-ending catastrophes.

My goal for this chapter is that you take specific learnings and mistakes to avoid. I also hope you learn from the process I went through as you reflect on your own journey. This should help you quickly get back up on your feet after experiencing inevitable failures. Whatever you do, don't let them debilitate you and keep you from moving forward.

To succeed as a marketer, you'll also need to be thoughtful about advancing your career, building a team, and working with peers. These crucial skills are the subject of our final chapters.

CHAPTER 9

CHART YOUR OWN PATH

"If opportunity doesn't knock, build a door."

—Milton Berle

My stage name was Udini. My friends (and children) love making fun of me for it so why should they be the only ones in on the fun? About a decade before I launched my marketing career, I was working as an amateur magician, performing in front of audiences all over Israel, where I grew up. I even had a couple of appearances on national TV. I was just an artsy kid, trying to find my way.

For years, I dabbled in puppetry—in most of my podcast interviews online, you can see Kermit the Frog behind me and the rest of his friends from *The Muppet Show*. I played music, and I did magic for 10 years as a stage magician. I performed illusions like levitating people and sawing them in half. I performed at hundreds of birthday parties. When I got into music, I played on the wedding circuit, at hotel receptions, and with some really talented, fun people.

I got into every aspect of performing arts I could, including stage lighting and sound control for dance and theater. I went to a high school for the arts, so I helped my friends with their the-ater, movie, and dance productions, and was heavily involved in the music department. I took on as many projects as I could and was completely captivated by the performing arts.

Growing up in Israel, though, everything changed when I turned 18 and had to join the army for four years. That experience gave me a lot of perspective. I started asking, *Where do I want to be as an adult?* I realized that even the most talented musicians I played with—the A-list musicians in Israel—were struggling to make ends meet. They'd go from one gig to another.

It's no different for performing artists in the United States. Unless you're in the top tenth of a percent—like a Taylor Swift—you're likely juggling multiple gigs: playing in an orchestra, teaching in the afternoon, then doing a chamber music concert on the weekend.

I realized I wanted a more stable life with a predictable income. I needed a grown-up job, but I also wanted to carry forward all the passions I had. One of my first meaningful roles was as a Product Manager at a company without a marketing function. I found myself straddling this fence between customers on one side and the engineering team on the other.

Product management is fascinating because you have to speak two very different languages. You translate customer needs and expectations into engineering language, explaining what they like, what they hate, and what they expect. Then, you turn around and explain to customers—using their language—all the amazing things the product can do. You don't talk about bits and bytes, which excites engineers. You talk about benefits, transfor-mation, and what the product can do for *them*.

I realized I enjoyed the customer side of that game much more than the engineering side, and that's when I decided to pursue a career in marketing. Honestly, if you look at my background—from magic to music to puppetry—it all ties together in marketing.

Marketing is really just putting on a show. It's the business form of the performing arts.

One way I like to describe marketing is as creativity in service of capitalism. We're being creative, crafting experiences, and making people feel something. At the end of the day, we want them to buy a product—whether it's toothpaste, a car, or revenue intelligence software. But the best marketing doesn't feel like selling. It makes people *want* to buy because they connect with the brand, the vibe, and the experience.

Having fun and putting on a show resonates with people. It's a different style of marketing that brings out personality and creates an adventure. For example, I once emceed a Gong event in a red velvet smoking jacket while sitting at a piano. One of my colleagues was dressed in a glamorous evening gown, making it a night to remember.

I love basking in that energy—people coming up to me after a webinar, podcast, or dinner event, saying, "That was different; I've been to a hundred events, but this was one of the best." That feedback is everything to me. I truly see my current career as a reincarnation of my childhood passion for the performing arts. A heartfelt word of appreciation from a colleague or attendee is the closest I'll come to a standing ovation.

Now that my husband and I have three creative kids, I get to experience the joy of watching them grow and explore their own passions. We dress up in costumes every year for the holidays and I post our family photos on LinkedIn. I want my business network to know that you don't have to walk around in stuffy business suits pretending you're someone you're not. You can be unconventional and intentional about it—not to mention having a life outside of work.

No Role? No Problem.

I created my first VP Marketing role out of thin air.

Many years ago, I was the first Product Manager at a small company named Sarine Technologies. That meant I often had to step out of my formal role to accomplish what the company needed, including some light marketing, as the company did not have a dedicated marketing function at the time. After five years in my product role, which included increasing amounts of marketing work, I was ready to take the plunge. I approached my CEO, Zeev Leshem, and made my case.

"Look," I said, "I'm really enjoying my role as Product Manager, working with our internal engineering team and with our customers. I've been keeping the lights on for marketing but I think the company would grow faster if we had a full-time marketing function supporting our customers and prospects. We could accomplish so much more with better advertising, events, and marketing materials."

"Yes, I think you're right," Zeev agreed.

"Luckily, I have just the right guy for you," I grinned. "How about I start looking for a new Product Manager to replace me in my current role and after they are fully in seat, I'll take on the new VP of Marketing role?"

"Well played, Udi. Let's do it!"

I went on to hire David Block, a young Product Manager who took over my role and allowed me to take on the newly created role of VP of Marketing. My first full-time marketing role, which I had created out of thin air by advocating its importance to the company, before offering to fill it. The bet the CEO took on me worked out well: the company grew quickly and had a nice IPO on the Singapore Stock Exchange (SGX).

David also proved himself in the best way imaginable: he did a great job and quickly climbed the ranks, eventually becoming the company's CEO when Zeev retired.

I discovered I love carving out new roles for myself so much that I kept doing it, taking on four other companies' first VP of Marketing role. At Gong, I transitioned into the role of the company's first CMO, and several years later, I became the company's first Chief Evangelist.

My point is you can absolutely carve out your own role, as I did. It takes some confidence in your strengths and areas of passion, as well as advocating for yourself and putting the good of the company ahead of your own.

Show, Don't Tell

Solving problems outside of your formal domain and taking work off your manager's table demonstrates you're ready for your next role. Somewhat counterintuitively, most people earn their promotion *after* they've demonstrated they're operating at the next level and not the other way around.

Tricia Gellman started out as a Business Development Manager. She joined Apple as an evangelist for the graphic designer community and developers of graphic design tools. Six weeks into her new job, a reorganization happened and she was transferred into marketing. "I was devastated because I thought marketing was a total waste of time," she half-joked. "But I quickly got involved in very impactful work—speaking at conferences and driving conversations about the future we were shaping." That landed her a director-level marketing job at Adobe. Tricia moved on to become an influential CMO.

Few marketers studied marketing in college. Unlike other disciplines, such as finance, law, and engineering, most marketers I know stumbled upon their profession and do their best to learn as they go and carve out their personal career paths. This makes marketing an exciting profession because you can often write your own story, but it also makes it a challenging career path, as it isn't as well-paved as some others.

Carilu Dietrich went down several such paths. She was on a marketing team at a company that was acquired. She wasn't getting along very well with the CMO, so she went to her general manager and pitched a job that didn't exist. As a result, she was made responsible for all aspects of the acquisition integration across the company, bridging the gap of people, processes, and technology between the two merged companies.

"Because I worked with so many people, I ended up getting a great role in the fastest-growing product of the parent company and making great connections," she explained. Then it happened again. "When another one of my companies got acquired by Oracle, I pitched myself for an advertising role I'd never done before and got it based on my versatile track record and technical chops. It became my favorite job." Pushing herself outside of her comfort zone paid off in spades.

"Chance favors the prepared mind, and opportunity favors the bold," said Louis Pasteur. Paradoxically, to earn your next career break you'll need to demonstrate you can operate at the next level. Then, when opportunity knocks, open that door and march through it as if you own the place.

The One Thing Marketing Can't Fix

When Amit Bendov co-founded Gong, he called and asked me whether I would join Gong to lead its marketing. He had already beta-tested the product with 12 companies, 11 of which quickly turned into paying customers. While it was still very early in the life of the company, it wasn't until they had achieved that initial product-market fit that Amit began to think about marketing.

Most marketers do well only once their company has achieved some level of product-market fit (PMF). A product has PMF when it solves a significant problem for customers and is positioned to meet their needs. Typically, startup founders are under pressure from investors to get the company off the ground. They might have a handful of beta customers evaluating the initial product.

What do some CEOs do? Bring on a marketing leader to create market traction. But all too often, this happens before there's a clear value proposition to offer intended customers and a product that satisfies that proposition.

The result? The CMO fails to achieve their goals and ends up losing their job. The CEO blames it on the CMO's incompetence, who leaves deflated and defeated, resenting the company that needs to get its act together.

Why does this happen?

A startup marketer is regularly asked to be a Jack or Jane of all trades: build brand awareness, generate demand, create an industry category, craft compelling messaging, and more. But there's one thing marketers can't fix.

I suspect it's the top reason startup CMOs lose their jobs. I've personally made the mistake of not performing due diligence on this before joining a company, and I've seen my peers make the same mistake. It's a major factor that can cause marketers with the best track records to fail.

Product-market fit. That elusive, make-or-break state of a company and its product. There's just no way to succeed without it. Crafting the right messaging for the best of products is hard enough. Coming up with a persuasive story for a product no one really needs or understands is impossible.

Generating a predictable flow of qualified opportunities can feel like a miracle even at A-list companies. But trying to get senior executives to suppress yawning for 45 minutes at a boring demo of a half-baked product? Professional suicide.

Anthony Kennada, a serial CMO and entrepreneur, experienced this firsthand. Two of his first seven employees were marketers. Both were early in their career, a generalist and a content marketer. They were trying to build an audience and then sell them the product. They did a good job building excitement around the company in general but the product did not fulfill that excitement. "We simply didn't have product-market fit. I took on being acting CMO because our lack of PMF was holding back my team and they were not set up for success," Anthony recalls.

On the opposite end of the spectrum, Dave Gerhardt was the first marketing hire at Drift, a Conversational Marketing company and a category leader in its time. Dave recalls, "When I joined the company, we didn't have product-market fit. We started building an audience and a community of product marketers, knowing that eventually we'll build a product for that audience." The insights gleaned from that community led Drift to build a product that ended up being used on more than 100,000 websites.

But Dave is an outlier. Most marketers are far more likely to succeed while scaling marketing for a product that's already achieved basic product-market fit.

Sniff It Out

There are several tell-tale signs of product-market fit—or lack thereof—marketers should look for when considering a startup position and CEOs should consider when deciding on when to bring in a marketing leader.

If the company has customers, go talk with them. Ask them how happy they are with the product and how it's transformed their business. Read their online reviews of the product and ask to see their Net Promoter Score (NPS).

If the company doesn't have customers, find out how long the company has been working on its product and what efforts it has made to acquire customers. If dozens of reputable companies have refused to trial the product, that's a warning signal. Talk to a friend who could be a potential user of the product, and get a sense of how excited they are about the product's benefits.

What are the company's customer churn and retention rates? A high churn rate and low retention rate could indicate a product-market fit problem.

What do employee retention and attrition look like? Great team members stay just long enough to figure out that the problem is PMF before they leave.

Has the company been struggling to secure funding? Sharp investors are usually good at spotting good and bad PMF potential.

If one or more of these warning signs exists, it's probably too early for a head of marketing to make a real impact. Bringing in a marketing leader before minimal, viable product-market fit means setting everyone up for failure.

Unless you have proven experience and passion for helping the team achieve product-market fit—which most marketing leaders don't have—it would serve everyone's best interests to wait until the founding product team can capture stronger signals of PMF before expecting a marketing leader to scale demand generation and brand awareness.

Picking the Right Company

Once you've confirmed the initial PMF, the next risk factor to clear is your future manager, typically the CEO. A huge part of your success depends on how your CEO values you and gets along with you. Working for a CEO who understands and has realistic expectations of what marketing can achieve will make your job not only easier but also more enjoyable.

To be clear, this doesn't get you off the hook of articulating to the CEO and your peers the logic behind your plan and transparently communicating both successes and failures. But for some CEOs with a misunderstanding of what marketing can and cannot do, that won't be enough.

To get an idea of how a CEO thinks about marketing, consider asking questions like, "What does success in my role look like?" so you can gauge whether you're both aligned on what's doable and whether you're the right person to achieve it; or, "Tell me about a great marketer you've worked with—what made you value them and how did they achieve success?" which will give you hints to the behaviors and results your potential CEO values.

Dave Gerhardt has had mixed experiences with his prospective CEOs. He declined to work for a company selling to educational institutes because his vision for marketing was too distant from that of its CEO. At Drift, he had the opposite experience. He learned early on from a podcast interview he conducted with the CEO that they thought about marketing in similar ways. "I wanted to work with him because we gelled so well," he recalls. Dave went on to work two different stints at Drift for nearly five years.

Once you land your new role at the right company with a kickass CEO, you're ready to make a powerful impact. Let's turn our attention to devising "a big idea" strategy, taking a stand on issues that matter, and paying it forward by helping others climb the ladder.

CHAPTER 10

LAY THE FOUNDATION FOR GREATNESS

"Dreams and big ideas are plentiful, but few people have the courage to realize their ambitions."

—Touker Suleyman

"It's amazing to see a visible LGBT executive in tech. That reminds me I can make it happen!" Ricky messaged me on LinkedIn.

Soon after Ricky's message came through, I received similar messages from others in my network. Jason wrote, "Thank you for posting during Pride and continuously for the LGBTQ+ community. As a gay man, I appreciate those who pave the way so I just wanted to say thank you!"

Then Mike chimed in, "It's very encouraging to see an exec at a great firm like Gong also be vocal and bring attention to these topics. Thank you!"

Earlier that day, I had posted a photo of my family marching in the San Francisco Pride Parade. A few years ago, I would have kept family photos like this for social networks like Facebook, but I came to realize that business networks are the perfect place to take a stand on important global and social issues.

135

This is just one of the ways you can use your position of power for good. In this chapter, we'll discuss ways to advance your career and help others on their way.

But first, let's talk about the "S" word.

The Big Idea

Great marketing campaigns start with a dirty 8-letter word that many like to dodge—*Strategy*.

First, let's define what it's not: a laundry list of campaigns and programs is not a strategy.

A common mistake I've made, and seen many others make, is rushing into marketing execution—campaigns, programs, and events—without devising and agreeing with your peers on a clear strategy first.

Your chosen marketing strategy can be difficult to achieve but should always be simple to articulate. There should be a straightforward way of describing what success will look like. Then work your way back to create the strategy.

It's useful to have a "big idea" for your overall strategy and for smaller components of it, like trade shows (why will people line up at your booth?) or content assets (what will make them download it?).

Ask yourself, "What's the big idea?"

If you can't easily explain it, you haven't found it yet.

A simple yet effective way of formulating a strategy your CEO and peers will get excited about starts by looking at the high-level company goals. Let's say your company wants to achieve $1 million in sales this year. Your marketing strategy should clearly specify how it supports that goal so everyone around the boardroom table understands how you and your team are aligned with and supporting the company plan.

To do this, you'll likely start by breaking down the pipeline needs for achieving the sales goal. Then, you'll make some conversion-rate assumptions and set targets for various pipeline sources. Finally, you'll articulate a plan to achieve those targets.

Here's how you might articulate this strategy:

"To support our $1 million sales target this year, my team will create a $4 million pipeline. We expect half of that to come from content marketing, one quarter from events, and the remainder from paid ads and inbound traffic.

"To grow an effective inbound motion, we'll build valuable content based on what works in sales, according to our data. We expect sales leaders to consume and share this content with their peers, which will increase both inbound pipeline and brand awareness."

Tricia Gellman rocked this process during her time at Salesforce. The company had thousands of salespeople who weren't aligned with marketing, so she created a monthly communication cadence for sales and marketing.

For credibility among the salespeople, it was crucially led by sales leadership and the agenda was what both teams were going to do that month to make everyone successful. Tricia recalls agreeing on product launches, key messaging, lead lists to work on, and so on. "The sales leader kicked off the call, which sent a message to both teams on how important this process is, and then kicked it off to me to continue, which gave me a lot of credibility," she said. This is a shining example of sales and marketing alignment, which we will discuss in depth in Chapter 12.

The advantage of having a marketing strategy clearly tied to company goals, ahead of laying out the detailed execution plan, is twofold: your peers on the management team will understand the logic of your plan, making it more likely for them to partner with you on it; and you'll have an easier time explaining it to your own team, aligning them on the higher-level goals.

If every team member truly understands the "North Star" you are working toward, they can adapt their own plan accordingly when the original plan doesn't work out exactly as they had hoped. It also helps you quickly distinguish between ideas that advance your strategy and those that distract you from it.

Wear Two Hats

As a function leader, you're always wearing two hats. The first belongs to your functional role as the leader of the marketing team. You need to make sure the entire team has the resources, path, and motivation to achieve their targets and that they consistently hit them. Everyone has a bad quarter now and then, but you still need to create a clear pattern of success.

The second hat is that of a company executive. When other departments are dealing with challenges, you need to step in to see how you can help. Early in her career, Carilu Dietrich was running PR when one of the company's product marketers left the company just before a big product release. The company needed someone to get the messaging done, update the website, get a customer story out, and manage the beta release process.

So Carilu did it all, which earned her a ton of respect and trust from her peers. Her recommendation is to "raise your hand for tough challenges, even if you're swamped with other work." Doing this means people come to you with opportunities you never knew existed.

If you see a problem that doesn't clearly fall into any department's court—and this happens all the time—you remove your marketing hat, put on your executive hat, and do what it takes to drive a solution. You might be able to solve it on your own or you might need to rally others to solve it together. This could be as strategic as figuring out which market your company should sell into next or as mundane as where to put the employee bike racks.

I'll be the first to admit I didn't always get this right. For years, I favored my marketing team when I should have leaned more toward my executive peers. My team loved me for having their back, and I became intoxicated by the employee engagement surveys showing 100% satisfaction from my team members. In hindsight, I should have better served my executive peers with what they needed from me while making better hiring, firing, and promotion decisions on my team.

Master Your Craft

To earn your management's trust at a startup, you'll have to master your craft. You need to understand, beyond a basic level, what your team members are doing, why an email campaign succeeded, what to ask them if it didn't, and how to explain it to management.

This doesn't mean you need to be the best email marketer or a top marketing automation specialist, but you do need to know how to build the basic systems in the beginning, and you should be seen as a mentor and coach to your team members.

To be respected as a marketing professional, you need to know what you're talking about and ask the right questions to learn more.

It's easy to cop out of mastering your craft by hiring agencies and team members to complement your weaknesses but this strategy has several limitations. First, as an early marketer at a startup, you're absolutely expected to do the actual work.

The company is unlikely to have a large marketing budget so they assume you'll be doing a lot of hands-on work and not just coordinating external agencies to do it for you. Second, it will be much easier for you to attract ambitious talent to your team if they believe they can learn from your hands-on experience.

A healthy dose of curiosity goes a long way. You should be talking to other marketing leaders to stay on top of the latest trends, technologies, and methodologies working for similar companies.

You don't necessarily have to copy what others are doing, but you do owe it to your company to familiarize yourself with the modern tool set of your craft so you can pick the right tools for the challenges at hand.

Go Deeper or Higher

As you evaluate your career options, an important question to ask yourself is whether you want to go deeper or higher. Going deeper means becoming an expert in your field, such as a product marketer or digital advertiser. These specialized roles can be highly rewarding, offering satisfaction through mastery of your craft, continuous learning, and the ability to apply cutting-edge knowledge to your work.

While these roles might lead to a function-leading vice president position, they typically don't go much further—and that's perfectly fine for those who value staying hands-on and focused on individual contribution rather than shifting to more strategic oversight responsibilities.

Sometimes life pushes you in this direction: when I left a company due to a bad cultural fit between the co-founders and me, I had a toddler at home and we were expecting twins in the coming months. I quickly realized I wouldn't have the energy and focus needed to succeed in another leadership role at that time and consciously made the decision to shift into consulting for a couple of years, until the children grew older and I would get some of my time (and sleep) back. Those two years of consulting ended when I received the life-changing call from Gong's co-founder, Amit Bendov.

For other marketers, climbing up the corporate ladder is what truly excites them. They have their eyes set on being a CMO. There are great rewards attached to this role, especially if you're part of the company's C-suite of executives and get the compensation that comes with it. But here's a fair warning from Dave

Gerhardt, former CMO at Drift: "CMOs don't get to do a lot of 'real marketing' once their teams grow, so go on that route if you think you won't miss it too much. Otherwise, focus on what you love doing."

I confess I missed "real marketing" when I was managing a large team of highly specialized marketers. They didn't leave me much to do except manage strategy and align all team members and resources on our evolving goals.

The higher up you climb and especially as your team grows, you'll be doing less marketing and more general management: staff meetings, cross-functional partner meetings, one-on-one meetings with your direct reports, skip-level meetings with indirect reports, and so on. Many find this birdseye overview type of management satisfying but others miss the marketing work they did when they were more involved in the day-to-day operations.

Carilu Dietrich educated herself on all marketing functions to earn her CMO title: "I did everything in marketing: PR, advertising, product marketing, and demand generation," she said. Carilu believes cross-training is super important—know enough about everything so you can manage that function later in an informed way.

She loved seeing all the pieces of the puzzle and how they fit together. "Demand gen won't work without great messaging, PR is useless if it doesn't support a strong product strategy, and so on," she explains.

Deeper and higher are both good options, depending on where your passion lies and what type of work you're excited to fill your day with. It's also perfectly fine to change your preference between them as your life seasons change.

Take a Stand

I've met remarkable executives who prefer to keep silent on global and social issues, in fear of alienating some of their team members. I respectfully disagree with that choice. Today's workforce expects more than a salary and a cubicle from their employer. They want to feel part of an organization that shares their core values, which requires top executives and other leaders to speak up and voice their values when they come into question.

We saw an example of this when Disney fought against the State of Florida for promoting its "don't say gay" legislation. Companies like Google and Apple regularly sponsor Pride parades around the world and have large groups of employees marching in them. You might recall the Black Lives Matter snafu discussed in Chapter 8, which started with the best intentions but managed to enrage some of our customers.

Women's rights, Black rights, regional wars, and other social issues of this scale can be tough to tackle. The easiest thing to do is try to ignore them. But not taking a stand is often perceived as taking a clear stand, usually by both sides of the argument.

Instead of upsetting *every*one, you might as well take a stand and risk upsetting only those who strongly disagree with your point of view. You'll be doing a huge favor to those who share your views and are looking for senior voices like yours to act on behalf of those not yet comfortable enough to share them.

"I was a public relations person first," admits Carilu Dietrich. "So I'm sensitive to companies being careful about taking a stand because they do run the risk of alienating some of their customers who inevitably span the spectrum." But even Carilu agrees there are times when executives need to take a stand. It also depends on the beliefs of the CEO, the company's strength, and its likelihood to survive taking a stand on controversial issues, she adds.

If you're looking for a thorny debate, just ask folks about using executive power to speak up on global and social issues. Tricia Gellman, a serial CMO and advisor, illustrates this complexity: "I couldn't work side-by-side with other executives who are too far from my own values on major issues." Tricia believes that standing for something is more important than the customers she might lose as a result. Doing so is crucial also for recruiting GenZ and younger generations who expect it. She sums it up beautifully:

"If you don't share your views on hot topics, then who will?"

Eighty percent of respondents to the Edelman Trust Barometer[25] want CEOs to speak up and lead societal action. Nearly two-thirds of employees will only work at a company if they share the same values. This evidence should urge executives to weigh in and lead on societal issues.

Anthony Kennada, a serial CMO and entrepreneur, hesitantly agrees: "We can't ignore this data. People buy from people and want to work with peers with shared values. So execs need to

---

[25] Richard Edelman, "Companies Must Not Stay Silent," Edelman, February 3, 2023, https://www.edelman.com/insights/companies-must-not-stay-silent.

be vulnerable and share things publicly. Personally, I'm not sure where to draw the line." He thinks you should speak up despite the complexity of the world being divided on many of these issues. According to Anthony, there's corporate activism and there's doing the right thing by being authentic and vulnerable.

One thing's for sure, you can't sit on the sideline and be vanilla about everything. Even if not everyone agrees with your every opinion, Anthony believes we can create an environment of respect for different temperaments, talents, and convictions. He hopes we can welcome diversity of thought as long as it's within the bounds of decency, respect, and empathy.

As an openly gay executive, I've followed my own advice often: I celebrated my same-sex wedding at my workplace; every Pride Month, I post on LinkedIn something about the last year's achievements and challenges of the LGBTQ+ community; when Roe v. Wade was overturned by the Supreme Court, compromising women's rights, I immediately took to social media to express how appalled I was.

Every time I post something like this, I get many public comments as well as private messages, thanking me for speaking up on important issues and giving a voice to those who might not have one. Yes, I occasionally get some hate comments, too, but they are totally worth enduring for the larger benefits at stake.

Pay It Forward

As you establish yourself as an expert marketer, especially in a senior role, you'll be approached by earlier career marketers and CEOs looking for advice on their own marketing challenges.

While it might get to a point where you cannot entertain every single meeting request, you should do your best to spread good karma by devoting an hour or two each week to mentoring those who don't have your experience. Not only will this build your reputation as a generous and helpful professional, but it will also present you with new opportunities like full-time, board, and advisory roles, as well as speaking opportunities. These opportunities won't find you unless you open the door when they knock.

So far we've covered career moves you have relative control over like carving out your next role, showing you're ready for it, and picking the right company and CEO. Once you're in seat, you'll want to form a strategy, master your craft, and choose between going deeper or higher. As you gain seniority and status, you'll have the privilege of taking a stand on social and global issues and paying it forward.

But you can't do it all alone. To truly succeed in marketing, especially as you climb up the corporate ladder, you'll need to excel at building and managing a winning team. You'll also need to earn the trust of and work well with your peers, particularly in sales. These are the topics we'll explore in our final two chapters.

CHAPTER 11

BUILDING A COURAGEOUS TEAM

*"Talent wins games, but teamwork
and intelligence win championships."*

—Michael Jordan

Vince Chan was working on his cousin's Filipino food truck when he got the call that would change his life.

"Gong is producing a big event and we could use an extra pair of helping hands. Are you in?"

The caller was Russell Banzon, the Director of Demand Generation on my marketing team at Gong. In his spare time, Russell was the part-time director of a hip-hop dance company Vince was dancing with.

Russell needed help with our first Revenue Intelligence Summit, but didn't have an approved headcount he could hire for. So he got creative and hired Vince as an external contractor for three months, using the event budget he could spare.

"In a typical hiring process, someone like Vince, with no experience in tech or marketing would almost never get a shot at earning a full-time role," Russell admits. "During his time as an intern, we were able to vet him and explore his fit with Gong."

During his short internship, Vince found his way into the heart of every team member he encountered with his eagerness to learn and to solve problems, always with a can-do attitude and an infectious smile.

"I felt like Charlie getting the golden ticket to Willy Wonka's chocolate factory," he later shared in an emotional interview for this book. "Stepping into Gong's office, the energy felt surreal. I never felt like I was treated as just an intern, which really boosted my self-confidence. I was a 26-year-old who knew nothing about the tech industry and everyone was helping each other grow and achieve their goals."

When our big event ended with roaring success, Russell suggested we hire Vince for a full-time role to manage our social media channels, an area where Vince had no experience. If he had blindly applied for the open role, he would not have been invited for an interview, which would have been a huge loss to our team. But getting to know Vince during his short internship made it clear to everyone that he would figure things out.

"Let's do it," I agreed, foregoing a formal interview process.

His experience on the food truck and in dance gave Vince invaluable grit and a self-learning mentality. He went through multiple certifications to advance his skills and help him succeed at his job.

He remembers being asked to prepare his first slide deck to make the case for his full-time role. "I was scared to my core," he admits. "But the warmth and support everyone around me provided quickly made me feel very comfortable. At Gong, leaders felt like peers and friends, not some distant executives." Vince aced his presentation and got the job.

Vince went on to become a very successful marketing coordinator, earning multiple promotions and managing everything from social media to merchandise and marketing operations. I learned a double lesson from Vince and other great hires we made from untraditional backgrounds. First, hiring for potential over experience gives early-career professionals the break they need. And second, it enriches the company with out-of-the-box thinking, fresh energy, and perspectives.

Next time you're in San Francisco, you should try a California burrito at Señor Sisig, Vince's cousin's Filipino food truck. It's mind-blowing!

Hiring for Potential Over Experience

When faced with a hiring decision, it's always a good idea to *consider* hiring for potential over experience. I'm not suggesting potential should throw experience out the window every time. If you need brain surgery, definitely go with the experienced surgeon over the new kid looking for a break.

Thankfully, as marketers, we don't make life-or-death decisions very often, so we have more wiggle room. Some roles, like technical product marketing or pricing and packaging design, require an education or experience that really sharpens your tools over time. I would make sure a candidate has picked up enough experience before trusting them to run these functions on my team. The "tuition fee" of their learning on the job would be too expensive.

But for other roles, all I look for is someone with common sense, high energy levels—which I can't teach—and fast self-learning.

Vince was a shining example of all these qualities, as were other successful hires I made for roles in content marketing, events coordination, and social media management, to name a few.

Early Hires

B2B Marketing teams grow in different ways but typically end up comprising four functional teams: demand generation, product marketing, PR & communications, and brand & creative.

The most common hiring question I'm asked by first-time CMOs and CEOs is, "Which one should I start with?"

In an attempt to avoid the cliché "it depends" response, I've developed the following framework, which I believe provides good guidance to most startups incepting their marketing team.

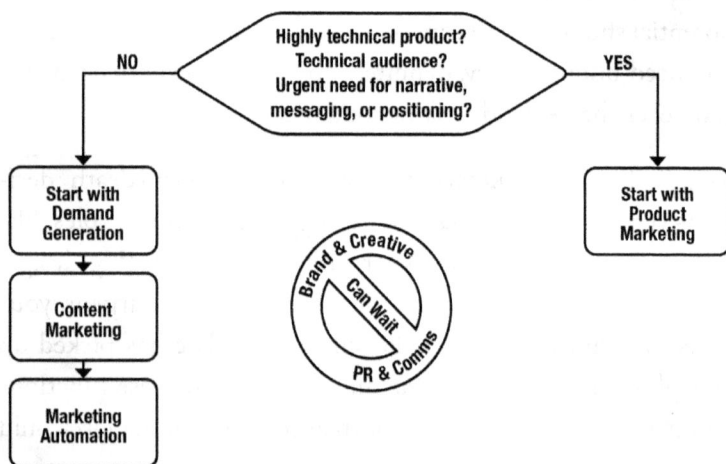

STEP 1: If you're an early-stage startup, PR and brand can almost always wait until a much later stage of your company's

growth. One exception is if design is *core* to your product and brand, like it is at Apple. I hired the first members of our PR and brand teams when Gong was at well over $100 million in annual recurring revenue (ARR). I didn't even hire a graphic designer until that stage, which blows most marketers' minds. We worked with great contractors and agencies for many years before succumbing to the overhead cost of full-time employees.

STEP 2: Figure out which is more urgent: demand generation or product marketing. My rule of thumb is to start with product marketing if you're selling a highly technical product, selling to a technical audience like engineers, or any other situation where it's clear you need a lot of upfront work on narrative, messaging, and positioning.

In almost every other situation, you'll want to hire a demand generation marketer first. As an early-stage startup, your days are numbered. Literally. Your investors want to see meaningful market traction before your next funding round. Generating demand that converts to sales demonstrates traction better than anything.

A fair question could be, "What if I need both?"

In that case, consider hiring one as your marketing team leader and the other as a function leader, reporting to the first. All marketing leaders end up being generalists as their teams grow, doing less specialized work and more overhead management. But in the early days of marketing, and especially until they make their tenth hire or so, the marketing leader should be a strong hands-on performer in at least one of these domains.

An ideal head-of-marketing candidate would have already served as a leader or deputy of a marketing team, owning one of the primary functions. You'll want to avoid taking a risky leap of faith in someone who managed only a smaller part of the team, like social media, and expecting them to run the entire team. From their previous vantage point, they didn't get a chance to see the full picture of how all marketing functions work together to achieve their goals.

There's a chance that person learns quickly and figures it out, but they would be better set up for success by climbing the ladder one rung at a time, advancing into a functional leadership position before becoming the circus ringmaster.

STEP 3: There are many specialties within the demand generation function: content creation, website, advertising, SEO, events, and marketing automation, to name a few. Some of these might later move into a shared services team. The right content marketer can make an immeasurable impact on your demand generation efforts. The first hire I made at Gong was a content marketer, and I would do it again. My best content marketers came from our buyers' domain: they were former salespeople I hired to create content for other sales professionals. This allowed them to write in an authentic voice that a generalist writer would have struggled to replicate.

STEP 4: A dedicated marketing automation person is a huge time-saver. Such was my second hire at Gong. She took a lot of grunt work off my hands and freed me to do more strategic work while she turned our lead-routing, website forms, and email campaigns into a well-oiled machine.

To summarize my thinking on early hires:

1. Set aside brand & creative and PR & comms. They should rarely be your first priority.
2. If you're selling a technical product, selling to a technical buyer, or know you'll need a lot of messaging work upfront, start with product marketing. Otherwise, start with demand generation.
3. A content marketer from your buyers' domain is often the best choice to start with when building your demand generation function.
4. A marketing automation specialist can take a lot of tactical work off your desk and free you for higher-value work.

Traits of a Great Team

I've been privileged to lead teams ranging from 1 to 60 reports. I've heard from my team members and seen for myself what made them thrive, succeed, and produce work broadly considered some of the best B2B marketing our industry has seen.

Three team operating principles made the magic happen:

1. Foster a Culture of Healthy Risk-Taking
2. Stay Involved Without Micromanaging
3. Keep It Simple

Let's take a deeper look at each one.

Foster a Culture of Healthy Risk-Taking

This principle counters the "playing it safe" approach, which often leads to stale, boring marketing. When a team member approached me saying, "I have a crazy idea I'd like your thoughts on," I immediately stopped what I was doing, and with a big smile on my face, said "I love crazy ideas!"

"It felt like you were pouring gasoline on the fire, and we were the ones a little hesitant at times," Chris Orlob, the first content creator on my team, remembers. "You were hard-driving us to take risks and be edgy."

Some of the best marketing ideas and campaigns came from my team members who felt the freedom to come up with unorthodox ideas and enjoyed pulling them off, whether or not they actually worked out. In his book *Think Again*, author Adam Grant calls this "Psychological Safety." It's the foundation of a learning culture, which allows people to raise concerns and ideas in a climate of respect and trust, without fear or reprisal.

Here are some fun examples:

Like most B2B websites, we had a standard chatbot with an uninspiring robot image. Vince Chan was responsible for making our chatbot more productive as a source of inbound demo requests, so he decided to swap out the robot image for one of Bruno, our bulldog mascot.

Noticing the chatbot change, I asked at a team meeting, "Who did that?"

Assuming he was in trouble, Vince raised his hand slowly while holding his breath.

"That was an amazing idea, do more of that!" I encouraged him.

Vince exhaled.

We continued to use Bruno's image on our chatbot for many years and "dressed" him up for every season and holiday with accessories and cheeky conversation starters like, "Woof! Who's a good boy?" leading to increased website traffic engagement with a real impact on our business.

Nicolette Mychajluk, whom I initially hired as a sales development representative and who later joined the marketing team, came up with the name for our first industry conference: Celebrate. She ran it by our CEO, who loved it. For years, it has served us well.

Every B2B company creates customer videos showcasing praise for their products, but our videos were different. At least, that's what our customer marketing team leader Sheena Badani says. "They used humor and were lighthearted, showing the human side of our customers, not just the boring business facts." And to what does she attribute the difference? Creative freedom.

The content & social media team experimented with pop culture memes, which were hugely engaging and earned us thousands of followers to whom we could later market our product.

In short, making team members feel safe to experiment led to many lessons learned and brought out the best in them.

Stay Involved Without Micromanaging

It's no secret that employees hate being micromanaged and most managers pride themselves on not doing it. So, who's doing all the micromanagement everyone hates? Learning how to be a resource to your team without regulating their creativity to death is a delicate balancing act essential to running a thriving team.

The devil really is in the execution details, as Peter Drucker said: "Strategy is a commodity, execution is an art." Everyday execution is about the details. You can't defend a team member's budget request to your CFO without being informed on why your team chose a certain vendor, what results they're expecting, and what impact that investment will have on the business.

Vince, who was in charge of growing our social media following, said, "We felt empowered to lean in and trust ourselves and each other to transform ideas into reality." While I gave them high-level guidance at the start of the quarter, I let them figure out how to grow the channel on their own. If they needed my help, they knew I was only a phone call away.

With bright eyes and a big grin, Vince shared, "We had so much fun racing to update the marketing Slack channel every time we hit 1,000 new LinkedIn followers." I love that he still takes pride in those early wins.

Despite being world-class professionals at what they did, my team members came to me for coaching and feedback on things as detailed as email subject lines, images for social media, and event ticket discounts they were considering.

To make sure they continued seeing me as a trusted resource to improve their work, I needed to be in the weeds of what they were doing, reference up-to-date benchmarks, and demonstrate I was still in touch with their craft. They appreciated knowing that I was there to help if needed, but I would always encourage them to go with their best judgment.

Jonathan Costet, who crafted some of the most effective emails we sent to customers, said some of his best learning moments happened when I "picked apart" one of his email drafts. He explained, "I never took the feedback as a personal attack but as a genuine effort to make our work better."

Wait, you might ask, isn't that micromanaging?

No, it's staying involved. My team and I brainstormed often on *what* we should do and then went our separate ways to figure out *how* to do it. I loved it when my team members showed me their work and asked for feedback.

When onboarding new team members, I clarified that they have my full permission to err a lot and that it's better that they do it quickly. I always prefer pulling back a "wild horse" than having to kick one in the rear end to get it going.

When a campaign delivered great results, I asked to see the details of what we did so we could learn from it and use it as a starting point for an even better future campaign. If a campaign didn't go as well as planned, I asked to explore what we could have done better. At these "postmortem" briefings, blaming fingers were rarely pointed.

Unfortunately, this management approach didn't work for all of Russell Banzon's team members during his tenure as Director of Demand Generation at Gong. He points out that you need to hire highly independent and proactive people who can work with the trust you put in them while you get out of their way. Some folks are going to need a lot more leaning in from their managers. Working this way is hugely freeing for the right people who are autonomous and seek feedback. Those without these traits did poor work on our team or required us to lean into places we shouldn't have.

When making a suggestion to a team member, even if I felt strongly about it, I reminded them, "It's your call." Because it truly was. And my team members learned quickly that I meant it. I didn't expect them to forget what they believed in and replace it with my advice. When in doubt, they should test out different ideas and see what works.

A friendly wager on a bottle of wine helped keep things interesting and fun. Nothing made me prouder than losing a bet to a team member whose idea outperformed mine. That's how I knew that person was advancing as a marketer and making sound decisions. Besides, we always ended up sharing the wine, no matter who won.

"It was exactly what we needed at the time," Sheena Badani said. She felt empowered to take ownership of her domain. Knowing she was trusted was why she gave her 100%. She loved the freedom to take risks without being micromanaged. "We weren't *following* a playbook, we were *creating* it," she said.

Keep It Simple

Going beyond the time-tested rule, my team not only kept things simple for us and our customers but also enforced a high-quality bar on everything we executed. The privacy notice email, which got shared on social media because customers found it brilliantly disruptive and entertaining, is a prime example.

In another experiment, we sent out an unconventional email invite to several thousand prospects. The email was written in plain text, with no HTML or images, and didn't contain any links, as most invitations do. The message informed the recipient that since they had attended a past Gong event, we thought they'd be interested in this early opportunity to join our next one, even before we launch the event's website or announce the speakers. Instead of the typical call-to-action in email invites, which sends recipients clicking through the email to a registration page and filling out a form before they can "Submit" it (what a dreadful name for an action that's supposed to be exciting!), we ended the email with: "Just reply to this email with 'yes' and I'll take care of your registration."

That email drove more than 700 registrants to the event and became part of our standard invitation protocol. By taking on the extra work ourselves, we made the registration process an enjoyable "no-brainer," which increased the number of those responding "yes" and attending our event.

Keep it simple.

Attracting Top Talent

If you ran a great campaign but didn't post about it on LinkedIn, did it even happen?

Sharing team learnings is a great way to attract top talent to your team. Sourcing and hiring great marketers is hard. One of the easiest ways of making sure the brightest minds in the industry come knocking on your door, begging to work on your team, is creating a well-known *team* brand. This might sound more complicated than it really is.

One thing my team and I did often, to drive a stream of top candidates, was post our learnings on LinkedIn. Since we were already doing postmortem campaign analysis for our internal needs, writing a quick blurb about the main learnings and posting it on LinkedIn usually took less than five minutes.

Those posts[26] regularly got a lot of engagement, including marketers tagging their peers to get their attention or opinion on our learnings. This exposed many talented marketers to our work and drove them to message us about our job openings they were hoping to fill.

To take this idea to the next level, consider writing detailed blog posts and presentations about your team's work, which you can share at industry events. Conference organizers love real-life stories and learnings grounded in useful takeaways that audience members can start using immediately.

Other CMOs often told me they shared my team's learnings with their own teams for inspiration, which both elevated *their* work and increased *our* team's brand, making it easier to attract top talent.

* * *

As a marketing leader, you are expected to hire, motivate, retain, and promote individuals who make up a winning team. This means starting with strategy while guiding the team through

---

26 Udi Ledergor, "How Gong Grew from Zero to Hundreds of Millions in ARR," LinkedIn, January 30, 2024, https://www.linkedin.com/feed/update/urn:li:activity:7158143285604020225/.

execution. Look to hire for potential over experience when viable and everyone will benefit.

Use the four-step formula to determine your first hires. You'll usually start with demand generation and product marketing, their internal order based on your target audience and product complexity. To keep the team motivated and on track to hit goals, foster a culture of healthy risk-taking, stay involved without micromanaging, and keep things simple.

Sharing your team's learnings on social media, blog posts, and at industry events will help you attract top talent who wants to work with like-minded peers. Telltale signs that your efforts are working are great folks within your company and others inquiring about working with you; team members winning industry awards; getting invited to speak at marketing conferences; and getting interview requests for podcasts, webinars, and blogs.

Last but not least, you and your team members will get a constant flow of job offers from other companies' CEOs, venture capitalists, and recruiters who will mention the great work you and your team are known for.

How you manage your team carries a lot of weight in your success as a marketing leader. But the often-overlooked yet equally important success factor is how you work with peers on the management team. Without a doubt, the peer most crucial to your success is the sales leader. Let's turn to our final chapter to learn how to effectively align with the sales team.

CHAPTER 12

YOU'RE HALF OF A TWO-HEADED DRAGON

*"If everyone is moving forward together,
then success takes care of itself."*

—Henry Ford

"Ryan, how do you take your coffee?" I asked.

Ryan Longfield, Gong's Chief Revenue Officer (CRO), and I had a long-standing habit of meeting once a week to discuss sales and marketing alignment issues. But instead of sitting down in a meeting room, we often took a short walk together that inevitably ended up at a nearby coffee shop, where we had a sweet ritual of sharing a cookie. Eavesdroppers would often hear us—two grown men—debating whether to split a chocolate chip or a halva cookie.

We'd pick up our beverages and half a cookie each, take turns paying for them, and then stroll back to the office while checking in on each other's personal lives and addressing any outstanding issues our teams were dealing with around staffing, quota attainment, organizational structure, and anything else that happened to surface that week.

I'm not exaggerating when I say our humble coffee runs did wonders for Gong's business performance as they ensured sales and marketing were always aligned, like a two-headed dragon, working in sync. I only had to ask Ryan once how he took his coffee. From that point on, we met often enough that we could order each others' beverages.

The simple act of jointly breaking bread (or a cookie) ensured we both knew what the other was struggling with and could calmly discuss how to tackle the issues at hand before we stepped into a larger meeting where fingers might have been pointed at each other. Not to mention how synchronized we appeared to the CEO and other executives, having discussed most outstanding issues in advance.

Sales and marketing have so much potential for friction. "Like when marketing bases its success on *quantity* (say, generating 1,000 leads) while sales needs them to be of high *quality* or we can't sell to them. That's a friction point," said Ryan. If salespeople are dying on the vine while marketing is celebrating their victory, it doesn't feel right.

Ryan was especially sensitive to how sales materials were made. The worst way of doing this, he said, is product marketing going into a room on their own and coming out with new messaging they expect sales to use. Developing sales materials in a vacuum, without sales and customer involvement, results in misalignment.

The idea that sales and marketing should work together like a two-headed dragon to ensure go-to-market success is not novel. Yet so many organizations suck at it. This can happen when marketers don't provide sales with the pipeline and sales materials it needs. I've even met marketing leaders too scared to reach out to sales, "because they seem too busy with more important things." This could be a sign of a marketer fearing they can't demonstrate how they're helping sales.

I've never seen a company with a successful go-to-market (GTM) motion that didn't excel in this alignment. Companies that get this right achieve their goals faster because everyone is rowing in the same direction and using each other as a force multiplier. To get it right, each team needs to deeply understand their role in the bigger GTM motion and play their part to ensure the machine keeps humming.

Nobody wonders what sales does.

Marketing doesn't enjoy that luxury.

Sales acquires new customers and expands existing ones. It's as simple as that. But far too often, sales leaders (and CEOs and CFOs) wonder what their peers in marketing are doing all day. They don't understand how marketing advances sales goals and what to make of all those vanity metrics like social media clicks and email open rates. How exactly do those contribute to sales?

"Marketing leaders need to get into the heads of sales leaders and step into their shoes," Ryan explains. "Imagine what it feels like to carry the weight of the revenue number. Working with great marketing leaders felt like they understood this dynamic and the pressure we're all under." It should feel like a team effort where sales and marketing share numbers and responsibility. They should all understand which metrics matter most to the other team.

So how does my CRO take his coffee, you might be wondering? Turns out he doesn't drink it at all. He takes tea.

Make Sales Easier

At Gong, we held monthly onboarding classes for each cohort of new Gongsters. During this two-week bootcamp, new hires met with several marketing leaders to better understand what we did and how we could help them succeed. My first slide in every onboarding presentation explained marketing's goal in three words: Make Sales Easier.

Since most onboarding classes included many new salespeople, they were now listening attentively. By telling them my team exists to help them succeed, they dropped their guard and any cynicism they might have come into the room with. They were intrigued with the myriad ways my team made sales easier through demand generation, increased brand awareness, category creation, and crafting sales materials.

Earning your sales peers' respect can be tough. "The best marketers and salespeople I've worked with deeply understood our buyers and the psychology of their buying journey," Ryan Longfield said. Sales interacts with customers every day and requires a similar level of market knowledge from our peers. Marketers who obsess themselves with understanding their buyers and markets will do better in their jobs and quickly earn the respect of their sales team.

Tricia Gellman, a serial marketing leader, also believes that marketing exists to warm the market for sales. Tricia cautions marketers against siloing themselves. Instead, she encourages them to align with sales. In her words, "Marketing needs a deep understanding of how the company makes money and should then pin itself on crucial moments in that process. For example, does the company use an enterprise or product-led sales motion? Each of these commands a different marketing plan. If marketing is siloed, it falls apart."

Like any healthy relationship, a good sales-marketing alliance relies on trust and communication. Trust is built over time with open communication. Leaders who share not just the good news, but also the bad and the ugly, are more likely to earn their peers' trust.

Practicing this takes effort and mistakes happen but can be redeemed. Let's take weekly pipeline meetings, as an example. If you're going to call out someone for not doing something well, the first time you do that should be in a private call. If you do make the mistake of calling them out in public, pick up the phone and apologize immediately after the meeting. Don't walk around resenting someone or hoping that they forget about it. Ryan and I did our best to adhere to this practice, which really reinforced our relationship.

The best way we've found to report bad news, such as insufficient pipeline, is:

1. What we know—just the facts.
2. Why we think it happened, ideally based on data.
3. What we're doing to fix it—an action plan.

Don't surprise your sales leader with bad news you could have shared earlier. If something isn't trending the way it should, make them aware of it early so you can tackle the obstacle together or at least know what you're getting into. Next, let's review actionable principles of aligning marketing and sales in practice.

Five Principles of Alignment

Most would agree that sales and marketing alignment is a good idea, but breaking it down into steps to achieve it can be tricky. Here are five things Ryan and I did to ensure our teams were aligned:

1. Share common Key Performance Indicators.
2. Agree on key definitions.
3. Unify reports and dashboards.
4. Meet regularly.
5. Invest in internal marketing.

Share Common KPIs

Ensure both teams' leaders share common Key Performance Indicators (KPIs) and how they are tied to compensation. For example, if sales leaders' compensation relies on hitting the company's revenue goals, which it almost always does, then senior marketing leaders should also have variable compensation tied to achieving revenue goals. Don't underestimate the value of your peers in sales knowing that you and your marketing leaders are incentivized to achieve the same high-level revenue goals as they are. This will minimize sales leaders rolling their eyes at marketing "vanity metrics" because they don't see how marketing is helping to achieve their revenue goals.

Ryan adds that shared goals should extend beyond demand generation to product marketing, specifically to desired conversion rates between opportunity stages, where salespeople often struggle and great product marketing can help.

Agree on Key Definitions

The "currency" marketing passes on to sales (e.g., leads, sales meetings, or opportunities) is one of several crucial definitions both teams need to agree on. These include clarification of what the company's Ideal Customer Profile (ICP) is, what constitutes a qualified opportunity, etc. These definitions should be revisited quarterly as both teams review the results of qualifying these ICP personas, how quickly and at what conversion rates they are turning into customers, and whether anything about their definition should be expanded or narrowed to increase business predictability.

Misaligned definitions of qualified leads or opportunities are a common source of friction. For example, marketing generates leads from small companies while sales is looking to sell to larger businesses. Or marketing hires the right person but sales expects them to have a budget to spend this year, which they don't. This creates dangerous silos in which marketing might believe it is meeting expectations with a misguided metric like Marketing Qualified Leads (MQLs) while sales is wondering why they are wasting their time with unqualified prospects.

As a rule of thumb, sales doesn't care much about MQLs and other KPIs that marketing should track only internally. Sales wants to see a clear path between a qualified lead and doing business with them, which is why I always advise against using

MQLs as the currency passed between the teams. A much better currency is a sales-qualified lead or opportunity, whose definition both teams agree on.

Our beloved VP of Sales, Jameson Yung, joked about this often with marketers, saying, "You brought us MQLs? That's adorable!"

Unify Reports & Dashboards

Create a unified set of reports and dashboards both teams understand and find valuable. These should be used on a weekly basis, if not more frequently, to assess how everyone is pacing toward their targets. If you follow the previous steps and have common definitions of your ICP and qualified opportunities, these shared reports should be easy to whip up so everyone understands where gaps exist and the teams can work together to bridge them instead of arguing over the underlying data.

Meet Regularly

Integrate both teams using recurring meetings and check-ins. For example, demand generation marketers should sit in weekly sales meetings to understand what their peers are struggling with and how marketing can help. Leaders on both teams and at every level of seniority should regularly check in with each other to discuss progress and help needed with pipeline and revenue. For instance, event managers should meet with sales reps whose prospects would make great attendees at an upcoming event and equip the sales team with compelling materials for inviting their contacts.

When an inbound sales development leader departed Gong, Ryan needed some time to find a replacement. I asked Russell

Banzon, my director of demand generation at the time, to step in and manage the sales development team for a quarter or two until we hired a replacement. This would ensure we didn't skip a beat on our pipeline-creation targets, as the inbound sales development team was a crucial part of that effort. With his always-positive attitude, Russell agreed to take on the extra work.

"Stepping into this role forced a new partnership on me and the other revenue leaders," Russell recalls. "My alignment with Ryan got deeper through working together on this part of the business." Their partnership continued long after Russell no longer ran the SDR team.

Ryan vividly remembers Russell's bold move: "It was totally atypical and took a leap of faith from us to give Russell the SDR team. He was so selfless about taking on this additional responsibility and quickly earned our trust." The interim role gave him a better understanding of how SDRs work and align with marketing. Our entire GTM process became a lot more streamlined as a result.

Invest in Internal Marketing

To ensure everyone understands how marketing is impacting pipeline creation and brand awareness and how others can help marketing make an even bigger impact, you should invest in internal marketing.

An illustrative example is when marketing asks sales to invite customers and prospects to a marketing event. Ryan emphasizes the mutual trust needed to pull this off. "When marketing asks sales to invite people to their events, they might not fully understand how hard it is to get these senior folks to show up. It's impossible to do without a good understanding of what value they'll be getting at the event." After marketing "smashes" 10 events, shares the results, and builds trust, it will get easier to get sales to send out the invites.

When the company's CEO or CRO gives kudos to the marketing team in an all-hands meeting or Slack channel, saying something like, "Thanks to our amazing marketing team for driving 200 attendees and influencing $3.5 million of pipeline at last week's event," makes a big impact. You don't need to wait for this to happen naturally. Good marketing leaders feed their CEO and CRO information that's easy to share on what they did, how it's helping sales, and what others can do to drive more impact, like inviting their contacts to an upcoming event or sharing a content piece on social media.

During his time at Drift, Dave Gerhardt met with his sales leader every day to understand what's happening in sales conversations, what's working, and what needs to change. "We had a culture of 'show and tell.' Every Friday, each team presented for five minutes on what they'd worked on that week, where they were on targets, and what they did to get there." That simple act of sharing plans and results did wonders for cross-team alignment.

How well you align with sales is one of the single biggest success factors for any CMO. But it goes further than that. You need to be a trusted partner to other business functions like customer success, finance, and sales operations, among others. Creating raving fans of all your cross-functional business partners will give you a seat at the proverbial table. It will also increase executive trust in you and your team's judgment, which will make it easier to secure resources and approve promotions you recommend.

To recap how marketing & sales can work together like a two-headed dragon:

- Demonstrate to sales and other stakeholders marketing's commitment to making sales easier.
- Nurture a strong relationship between marketing and sales leadership at all levels.
- Practice principles of great alignment, including sharing common KPIs, agreeing on key definitions, unifying reports & dashboards, meeting regularly, and investing in internal marketing.

The bottom line? Make sales easier.

BUILDING YOUR COURAGE

"Nobody got anything great by playing it safe."

—Shonda Rhimes

I am often asked what's the one thing or quick hack I attribute my success to. I ultimately disappoint when I explain the many steps I took to build my professional career, the inevitable failures, the ideas that never got off the ground, and the successes that earned my reputation.

Working with many companies, I've seen all the big reasons B2B marketing fails: from lack of product-market fit, through death by committee and ignoring the long game, to playing it safe—the riskiest strategy of all.

I did my best to place myself in supportive environments with extremely smart, hard-working people and to stay keenly aware of these pitfalls so I could choose a different path. But my journey hasn't been all sunshine and rainbows. Some of my best ideas never materialized—like placing our product in a Netflix series or creating a reality show for sales leaders.

Others got off the ground and flopped, like our efforts posting on social media channels outside LinkedIn or sponsoring a world-class golf tour. Even our second Super Bowl commercial, which cost three times more than the first, failed to generate the buzz we'd hoped for. But every failure was a learning moment, and we pressed on.

Our first Super Bowl ad, however, was a different story. It was a quirky reflection of the pandemic-era office culture in 2021. Punching above our weight really paid off because it wasn't just a 30-second spot; it was part of a larger narrative. It reflected our brand's personality and evolution, the maturity of our category, and the amplification power of our raving fans. I never owned the brand nor could I. It was the hundreds of Gongsters who lived and breathed our operating principles every day. Together, we turned our vision into a reality, creating moments of delight for customers, which generated invaluable word of mouth.

When we considered building a category at Gong, we knew the odds were against us. Most category-design efforts fail due to the massive effort of educating the market. But we focused on the huge payoff of getting it right: creating a line item in our buyers' budgets and defining the category narrative for years. The market Gong operates in continues to evolve but the Revenue Intelligence category we pioneered served us extremely well for years. It wasn't easy, but the courage to try made all the difference.

To create engaging content marketing, we ensured it was hyper-relevant to our audience, interesting and timely, and immediately applicable. We checked off the important boxes for packaging and distribution—and got hundreds of thousands of followers and subscribers to amplify our content in the process—thus increasing its reach. We had created the perception of being much larger than we were.

Our event experiences—whether we were blowing bubbles at trade show booths or fogging the stage at our own conference—created memorable moments customers would recall for years to come.

All these marketing tactics wouldn't have been enough if I hadn't been thoughtful about advancing my career, building an amazing team, and aligning with sales like a two-headed dragon.

Knowing 11 of Gong's 12 beta customers became paying customers as early as they did gave me the confidence to pick Gong for its product-marketing fit. Having worked with him twice before made it easy for me to pick a CEO who valued and challenged marketing in the best way possible. I can honestly say I owe a huge career debt to my long-time CEO and friend, Amit Bendov.

To build a winning team, I hired for potential over experience whenever it made sense, leading to remarkable results and helping young marketers establish their careers. I fostered a team culture of risk-taking, involvement without micromanaging, keeping it simple, and attracting top talent by showcasing our team's best work. Together we created what many of my team members described as the best years of their career.

Understanding my CRO's preference for tea over coffee may seem trivial, but small details like this have made an outsized impact on my career. Ryan Longfield, Gong's CRO during my CMO tenure, always knew marketing's goal was to make sales easier, and that alignment made everything smoother and a lot more fun for all of us.

As a marketer or startup founder vying for attention and growth, you'll succeed if you build up your courage and your team's to boldly be different, punch above your weight, chart your own path, and dare to be controversial and polarizing.

Courageous marketing isn't about chasing the latest trend or copying what's worked for others. It's about taking risks, learning from failures, and staying true to your unique vision. Remember, marketing is creativity in service of capitalism. It's about creating moments that make people want to buy because they connect with your brand, your vibe, and your experience.

My hope is that this book has given you the tools, inspiration, and courage to blaze your own trail, create meaningful impact, and achieve the career success you deserve.

Courageous Ideas

To help you create courageous marketing, I asked my team members and leading CMOs for a quick tip you can use *today*. Nothing fancy like building a category or planning a large event. All these ideas are easy to experiment with and the results could surprise you.

- "Know your audience, be your audience, and take risks. Learn how they think and speak, then write clearly and succinctly. And surround yourself with smart people— you never want to be the smarter person in the room." —*Vince Chan*
- "Don't celebrate marketing victories that don't feel like victories to sales. Make sure to demonstrate how the victory actually helps drive pipeline or sales." —*Ryan Longfield*
- "Look at the subject line of your next marketing email and the headline of your next landing page. Do they

deliver a clear, differentiated point of view? If not, rework them. Also, if you need more than one pizza box to feed a team working on a marketing campaign, there are too many people in the room. Reduce the team size to avoid death by committee." —*Russell Banzon*

- "Question what your team is currently working on. How will it advance your higher-level goals? How will it help sales? Shrink your plan to the essentials that will make an impact." —*Dave Gerhardt*

- "Once a week, listen to a customer call or talk directly to a customer. The closer you are to what your customers think, say, and want, the better your marketing will be." —*Carilu Dietrich*

- "Recycle business-lost deals on a regular basis. Most companies neglect these highly qualified leads. For your marketing not to suck, you need to take a stand. Stand for something, have a point of view." —*Tricia Gellman*

- "Post on LinkedIn once a day but not about your product. Write about a problem you care about. Be consistent and write one thing every day. Be vulnerable to sound authentic." —*Anthony Kennada*

- "Spend as much time as you can with customers. Visit the websites of every player in your space and adjacent spaces and study how they market. You will find opportunities to shine." —*Sheena Badani*

- "Put one 'big swing' in your plan each quarter. It should be risky with a big upside. It will help you build a brand that stands out. Also, look for 'dead ends' in your marketing: use thank-you pages to offer another piece of content or an email subscription." —*Devin Reed*

- "Go create content for the sole purpose of creating value for your audience. Do it for a quarter, forgetting about MQLs and product promotions. Do it in your emails, videos, and social channels. You'll be surprised by how engaging your content will become and how easily you'll be able to monetize it later." —*Chris Orlob*

- "Talk to your top salespeople to get their feedback on the quality of leads they're getting. You'll learn a lot about your audience targeting and lead-qualification criteria. Also, look at your inbound demo trends, searching for blips on the radar. Then reverse-engineer them to understand what happened: was it a successful employee activation? A PR stunt? A TV commercial? Go do more of those." —*Jonathan Costet*

- "Read psychology books. External inspiration is just as impactful as your internal scorecards. Build time for external inspiration into your calendar. *Pixar Storytelling* is a great book to read through the lens of 'what story am I telling about myself as a leader?'" —*Michelle Taite*

Go ahead and take your pick. Run with one of these ideas each week and in a few months, you'll be a completely different marketer. You'll be creating marketing that truly engages your audience, drives demand, and increases brand awareness. Do it for long enough, and you'll be known for courageous marketing.

ACKNOWLEDGMENTS

"You should really write a book," I kept hearing from peers who interviewed me in fireside chats and on podcasts. I knew I was fortunate to collect a ton of helpful experiences but couldn't figure out a good time to crystallize my stories and get all the perspectives I wanted to include in telling them in a useful way.

Stepping into my role as Chief Evangelist at Gong in 2023 was the perfect opportunity to interview my peers and team members and document our experience in hopes of inspiring other marketers to find their courage and create awesome marketing.

I consider myself a decent writer of short-form content like marketing emails and social media posts, but writing a proper book was beyond what I considered myself good at. I was grateful to discover the *Manuscripts* writing program where Eric Koaster, Ilia Epifanov, and Alexander Pyles helped me create my first solid book draft.

While that first draft included my version of the story, I quickly realized that adding the perspectives of my colleagues and team members, who truly made the magic happen, would enrich this book beyond recognition. And boy was I right. Ryan Longfield, Russell Banzon, Vince Chan, Jonathan Costet, Sheena Badani,

Chris Orlob, and Devin Reed not only filled in crucial details but also uncovered stories and perspectives I had either completely forgotten or was never even aware of.

As I reverse-engineered what worked for me and my teams throughout the years, I wanted to challenge my thinking and conclusions by overlaying them with those of leading CMOs who I look up to. That's when I interviewed Tricia Gellman, Anthony Kennada, Dave Gerhardt, Carilu Dietrich, Michelle Taite, and Andrew Davies. Their sharp points of view forced me to rethink some of the nuances in mine, and the advice in this book is so much richer for them.

Lori Lynn made the book one thousand times better with her thoughtful editing, reading, re-reading, tearing my manuscript apart, and lovingly putting it back together more skillfully than I ever could. Shanda Trofe from Transcendent Publishing masterfully orchestrated the book's cover and internal design while patiently fielding hundreds of my newbie writer questions on the publication process.

This book is an outcome of my incredibly fortunate marketing career, which would have taken a very different course if it were not for my longtime career mentor and leader, Amit Bendov. I have been beyond lucky and honored to work with Amit at three different companies throughout the past 27 years, and it's more than safe to say that he instilled in me not only the love of clever marketing but also the courage to bring it to life. His repeated trust in me has changed the course of both my career and my life.

Finally, many of my intense career years would not have been possible without the unwavering support of my life partner and husband, Guy Ledergor. He has supported my every career move for almost 20 years and should earn a Nobel Prize for his infinite patience with me. Guy and our three children, Tom, Noa, and Adam, are the safe haven I return to after every business trip and at the end of every long working day. They are a constant reminder of what's most important in this world and the drivers of my courage to act accordingly.

ABOUT THE AUTHOR

Udi **Ledergor** is the Chief Evangelist at Gong, where he helped define and dominate the revenue intelligence category, taking the company from zero to hundreds of millions in revenue and achieving a multi-billion-dollar valuation. A five-time marketing leader at B2B startups, Udi is known for his bold, human-centric approach to branding and storytelling.

An author, speaker, mentor, angel investor, and board member, Udi is also a passionate advocate for startups, storytelling, and creating unforgettable brand experiences.

When he's not building brands, Udi enjoys whisky, music, and social activism. He lives in San Francisco with his husband, Guy, their three children—Tom, Noa, and Adam—and their menagerie of pets, including a cat, a bearded dragon, and a chameleon.

Look for more courageous marketing ideas from Udi at:

UdiLedergor.com

WHAT'S NEXT

Did *Courageous Marketing* spark new ideas for you?

Have you applied something creative you're excited to share?

You can help spread the word!

Here's how:

1. Leave an honest review on Amazon or wherever you purchased your copy.
2. Share the love on LinkedIn or other social networks.
3. Connect with me on LinkedIn and tell me about your courageous moves.

Reach out at linkedin.com/in/udiledergor/ or simply scan the QR code below:

Together, we can replace the dry, stale marketing that has dominated B2B for far too long. It's time for a bold and refreshing takeover. Let's put on a show!